A SKIRT AROUND DUNDEE
A WALKER'S GUIDE TO THE CITY

BY Cambella McMahon

Pumpkin Press Souvenirs

ISBN (10 digit) 0-9554490-0-6, (13 digit) 978-0-9554490-0-0

First Printing in 2006 by
Wm. Culross & Son, Coupar Angus, Scotland

Published by Pumpkin Press Souvenirs
(Scotland)
email: pumpkinpresssouvenirs@yahoo.co.uk

Previous page Once owning oodles of Victorian charm, the now disused Tay Hotel still holds a bewitching presence at the foot of Union Street. (It's previous name, '*Mathers Hotel*', can still be spied on the north-east gable.)

Right A post box inlaid into a stone wall in Constitution Road. If you look for them, such interesting features can be found elaborating the streetscapes.

contents

INTRODUCTION

DUNDEE IS AN EXTRAORDINARY CITY. IT WELCOMES ITSELF AS A GIANT VILLAGE: FRIENDLY AND PREDICTABLE YET PARADOXICALLY, ENERGETIC AND STRIKINGLY URBAN. Endlessly creative and imaginative the city has a need to prove itself - an obsession even - to discover itself, to grow and create its Utopia. And in its own modest manner, is attaining this. This book is about Dundee. Through these four personally constructed walks, it is hoped that a medley of the city's greatest and least expected achievements may be revealed. Ultimately, with each footstep taken, is an insight towards the very life and soul of Dundee. Over the centuries, Dundee's constant regeneration has created an ever changing landscape. An epoch began. Modernisation seemed the only way to toss the shackles of an unfair past and Dundee, to date, seems caught in this momentum. Out with the old, in with the new. The result however, is either a vibrant city of unexpected contrasts, or an unbalanced hotch-potch of architectural fashions and ideas - depending on your point of view. Only time will tell of Dundee's success at riding the wave of economic optimism and resurgent creativity, knowing that for each reinvention there is an obliteration of more than just bricks and mortar.

'Dawg'
sculpture.

What makes a city? Its architecture? Its influencing characters? Its heritage? Its cityscape? All of these; and of course it is the people within the city, that makes it tick, who keep it alive, with a cultural activity that they and visitors to it can relate to. Dundee's people are its '*asset*'; being, as commented by one local councillor, "*among the friendliest, most welcoming and most entertaining you'll meet*".

Samuel's Clock, at the corner of Reform Street, is Dundee's famous meeting place. The Hammermen Craft; which includes goldsmiths, watchmakers, clockmakers and jewellers, is the seventh in the list of the '*Nine Trades*' (Incorporated Trades) and can be traced back in documents to 1587.

The city is sizzling with people. Today, Dundonian's mingle with a new wave of tourist activity; remarking in curiosity at voices from towns, countries afar, like wide-eyed tribes-folk encountering strangers for the first time.

'*Summer in the city*' event.

Historically, Dundee has always been a city in a state of change: this itself is intriguing. This book aims to set the stage - of taking the walker not only through the geographic location, but re-awakening a time and place. Inspecting even the smallest relic of the city's past, often unnoticed in the daily hubbub, unravels a story. Only imagination can limit how you recreate the scene. Whether Dundonian or a visitor - enjoy!

MEDIAEVAL MEANDER

" Rats!

They fought the dogs and killed the cats,

And bit the babies in the cradles,

And ate the cheeses out of the vats,

And licked the soup from the cooks' own ladles, "

ROBERT BROWNING, (1812-1889) extract from, *'The Pied Piper of Hamelin'*

Browning's mother, Sarah Anna Weideman, was born in Dundee - at a house in the Seagate.

Opposite The Howff: offering quiet contemplation.

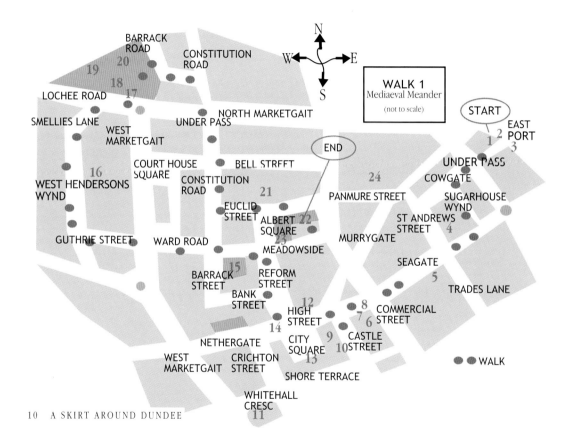

N

W — E

S

WALK 1
Mediaeval Meander
(not to scale)

START

BARRACK
ROAD

CONSTITUTION
ROAD

19 20

18
17

LOCHEE ROAD

SMELLIES LANE

WEST
MARKETGAIT

NORTH MARKETGAIT

UNDER PASS

EAST
PORT

1 2
3

UNDER PASS

COWGATE

SUGARHOUSE
WYND

COURT HOUSE
SQUARE

16

WEST HENDERSONS
WYND

CONSTITUTION
ROAD

BELL STREET

END

24

21

EUCLID
STREET

ALBERT
SQUARE

22

23

PANMURE STREET

ST ANDREWS
STREET

4

GUTHRIE STREET

WARD ROAD

MEADOWSIDE

MURRYGATE

BARRACK
STREET

15

REFORM
STREET

SEAGATE

5

TRADES LANE

BANK
STREET

12

HIGH
STREET

14

8
7 6

COMMERCIAL
STREET

NETHERGATE

CITY
SQUARE

9

13

CASTLE
10 STREET

WEST
MARKETGAIT

CRICHTON
STREET

SHORE TERRACE

WALK

WHITEHALL
CRESC

11

LEGEND

1	Wishart Arch		**13**	Caird Hall
2	Old Wishart Church		**14**	Public Art
3	Blackscroft Area		**15**	Howff
4	Sea Captain's House		**16**	Verdant Works
5	Plaque: Sarah Anne Weideman		**17**	Old Drinking Fountain
6	Cathedral Church of St Paul's		**18**	Old Time Gun
7	Statue: Admiral Duncan		**19**	Dudhope Castle
8	Plaque: William Wallace		**20**	Dudhope Park
9	Bust: William Shakespeare		**21**	Dundee High School
10	Tourist Information Office		**22**	McManus Galleries
11	Old Tay Hotel		**23**	Statues
12	Gardyne's Land		**24**	Dundee Central Library, Wellgate Centre

JUST BY WALKING THE STREETS FOR A DAY YOU CAN TRACE THE DEVELOPMENT OF DUNDEE'S HISTORICAL JOURNEY. ADDING TO THIS, BROWSING AMIDST THE ARCHITECTURE, streets and relics you can dig up an impression of the people and character of the town. Acting as a visual reference guide, this tour can be explored all at once or in stages - simply refer to the book and work at your own pace.

Begin in the Cowgate at the **Wishart Arch**, the eastern port of the old town. This city gateway, a remainder of the original city walls (which were erected in the 1590s to protect the town), probably served as a commercial toll for drovers who - described as *'marching self consciously along with stick in hand to keep the coos off the plennies'* - would enter the town with goods for sale in its regulated market.

Although the gate now stands isolated; during the Victorian era, this area once held a little romantic charm with cassies and gaslamps set between cobbled streets crammed with traditional stone tenements. Behind this affection however, was the reality of slums, of mostly one room and having no water supply or sanitation: rainwater was used for washing and drinking water was drawn from wells.

Mediaeval town gate - Wishart Arch: a much prized relic.

The Whishart Arch is named after the Protestant Martyr **George Wishart** (1514-1546), in honour of his having preached here. The legend of George Wishart and his connection to this structure probably ensured its survival and stands as one of only two remaining mediaeval town gates in Scotland - the other is the West Port of St Andrews.

Plaque: pinpoints the location of the Wishart Church.

Wishart was appreciated by the plague-stricken population of 16th-century Dundee whom he comforted and ministered to, and had become quite a '*local hero*'. Check the plaque, set into the arch, which credits his sanctity: '*during the plague of 1544 George Wishart preached from the parapet of this Port. The people standing within the Gate and the Plague-stricken lying without in booths*'. (Though in fact, whilst the Cowgate Port was not built in Whishart's lifetime, the legend remains.)

The story states that the religious establishment were suspicious of radical-thinking clerics and had become nervous about the activities of brave Wishart. The clergy led by the powerful Cardinal Beaton resolved to have him removed. The story continues that an attempt was made on Wishart's life near where the Cowgate Port stands but that he somehow survived it (and even helped his would be assasin to escape from the outraged mob). But in 1546, Wishart was betrayed into the hands of the Cardinal, and after a show trial in the Cathedral of St Andrews was burned at the stake outside the nearby castle. Legend says that Wishart held a '*bloody prophecy*' of Beaton's death - a prediction

Mains Castle is one of four castles situated within the city boundary, the others being; Claypots, Broughty Ferry and Dudhope (the latter two being encountered on the walks).

which was fulfiled two months later when a band of assassins gained entry to the very same castle and barbarously knifed the Cardinal to death.

From the stone arch, a step north-east will have you facing a stone building, there is a white plaque beneath the lintel of one of the three large curved windows which pinpoints the date as 1841. This identifys the **Wishart Church** which originally occupied the upper floor of the building, there being shops and a public house, the **John o' Groats** (c1850-1969) on the ground floor. In those days this combination of church and pub gave the building its characteristic nickname of '*Heaven and Hell*'.

It was from this church, that **Mary Slessor** (1848-1915) served as a helper to the poor of Dundee. Mary was a common mill lassie of '*red hair and fiery temperament*', who was later, in 1876, to become a missionary in one of the most savage areas of Africa. In Calabar, now part of Nigeria, the tribes indulged in child sacrificing, twin killings and other cruel rituals. Mary saved the lives of hundreds of native girls who would otherwise have been killed at birth, by adopting the babies.

Mary spent the rest of her life in Africa and when she died in 1915, she was known as *'The White Queen of Okoyong'*. Mary, who married a Nigerian and had two children Ayo David and Daniel MacArthur, is still highly respected today. In the McManus Galleries, (encountered later on the walk) you will find a devoted collection of paraphernalia depicting her life in Dundee and Calabar, including her mended spectacles and well loved bible.

Old-fashioned Dundee Drain-pipe detail: if you explore such curios can still be found - they may not be of great architectural quality, but always of architectural charm. From a building in Constable Street in the Blackscroft; an area which still maintains its industrial heritage.

Previous page 15 Clydesdale banknotes emblazoned with Mary Slessor's portrait and promise to pay the bearer £10. this issue was to circulate for a five year period.

Opposite Mary Slessor: section of stained glass windows, in the McManus Galleries - depicting her story from *'Millworker to Missionary'*.

Sally westwards, skirting the carpark and passing through the subway - turn second left into **Sugarhouse Wynd**. This pend is a remnant of one of the original lanes once running to the river before the reclamation of land for the sea-port began. The sugar-refining business was established here about 1770, and this wynd preserves the memory of an industry that has long become extinct in Dundee. A right turn access leads into an unexpected stone-cobbled nook.

Sea Captain's House: the restoration of this villa and the Calendering works behind it was the first major project of the Tayside Preservation Trust.

A simple stone villa stands in delightful isolation oblivious to the urban sprawl. This is the **'Sea Captain's House'** and dates mainly around 1770. It was owned by a *'maritime gentleman'* and the gardens would have originally stretched down to the River Tay. Later, when this was no longer considered a desirable place to live by its Georgian owners, the villa was absorbed into **William Shaw's calendering works** some time after 1822.

Staying - metaphorically - in this era, visualise this vicinity. Bustling with loaded carts full of sacks from the calendering mills, many a working horse would have stood patiently. Too great an opportunity for mischievous kids - they often used to play *'dare'* - to take a quick run and duck under the horse's belly. Amusing to watch, this ploy did not seem to bother the horses, though the carters were not very happy and the rascals were often rewarded with a flick of a whip across bare legs. This spot is so surrealistically set in time that you are whisked back some hundred or so years to the day. By night however (you have to be on the walk to appreciate this), on acknowledgement of its neighbours, assumes a different identity!

Turn right at the end of Sugarhouse Wynd and enter what was once the principle street of the mediaeval burgh - the Seagate. Note the **Pawnbrokers** on the corner at the crossroads; this is a revival of what once used to be an essential part of Dundee's working community. These businesses; once jostling among mills, loan-offices and second-hand shops, held no disguise, each one had the familiar logo of the three brass balls embellishing the entrance.

Pawnbroker's sign.

Pawnbroking was a simple way of raising money and the pawn shops were busy. Even though most people did not have items of much value, the broker would accept almost anything provided it was in a reasonably good condition and clean: women's shawls, bedclothes and best suits were popped in on Monday and redeemed by Saturday morning - in time for the football match in the afternoon. The transaction was always the same. The depositor would place the article on the counter and '*Uncle*' (one of many names given to the proprietor), once satisfied with the condition, would fix a price - there was no haggling, you could take it or leave it! When the customer nodded in agreement, a ticket was issued with terms and value and the time allowed to buy it back - with interest of course!

The Seagate was the location of the burning of Dundee witch **Grissel Jaffray** on November 11, 1669. In those days, witch prickers were hired and paid on commission for each witch they discovered. Jaffray was convicted of *'being in league with the devil'* and just before she was 'wirried' (strangled) and burned, she claimed there were other witches in Dundee, but no further executions took place. Jaffray lived in a house in Thorter Row in the old Overgate with her husband James. It was common for women and girls to practice superstitious rites; often connected with religious or agricultural festivals.

Beyond the crossroads, on the south side of the Seagate, there are two plaques set into the wall just yards from each other. One denotes the position of the original **Mercat Cross**; erected in the mid 13th century in the 'Seagait' or 'Highgait' and was the place where *'deals were done and announcements made'* before it was transferred to its location in the High Street. Incidentally, this site also contained the ancient tolbooth (Town House): where the courts and council met, where tolls and customs were collected, burgh matters administered and offenders imprisoned. The other plaque marks the birthplace in 1772, of **Sarah Anna Weideman**, mother of the poet, Robert Browning (1812-1889).

Above Pub sign of the former *'Grissel Jaffray's'* in St Andrews Street. In Scotland between 1560 and 1770 more than 4,500 people were killed as witches. Whereas in the middle ages, witches had been placated with offerings of oatmeal and milk, during this period they were seen as Satan's agents to be rooted out and killed.

'Model of Old Dundee': centre-piece of the McManus Galleries and Museum. (Photograph courtesy of McManus Galleries and Museum, Dundee.)

Sarah Weideman's father was the first manager of the Sugar-Refining Company (set up in Sugarhouse Wynd c1770) and was brought from Holland to control the business. Mr Weideman, who had a house built for him on the south side of the Cowgate, had two children: a son and a daughter. Sarah's brother, Captain Weideman, was a shipowner trading from Dundee who ultimately sold all his property and took his sister, to Clapham, London. Sarah then met and married Robert Browning (senior) and became the mother of the poet.

'To look up is to learn to love architecture'. This is a good maxim to apply to the **Cathedral Church of St Paul**, which looms ahead on Castlehill. Designed by **Sir George Gilbert Scott** (1811-1878) in 1853, it is one of two existing buildings in the city by the famous *'Gothic'* architect, the other is the McManus Galleries. The church soars skywards: the spire is 210 feet high and the surrounding steps and portal cause you to step back at the shock of its gigantic proportions. Austere, straight-laced even, is the exterior; but on the contrary, once inside - Abracadabra - you enter a family chapel, a candlelit holiness of ecclesiastical treasures and heritage. Definitely allow yourself a sneaky peak!

St Paul's Cathedral: the spire soars so high, you feel as though you have suddenly shrunk!

Dundee Castle once stood here upon the old Castle Rock where the church now rests. Unfortunately, there is no recorded picture of the castle, which was destroyed about the time of Bannockburn. Dundee's vital position on the main northern coastal route, and its importance as a defensible base for sea-born supplies, earned its castle numerous sieges and sackings. Legend says that it figured significantly in the War of Independence; was damaged by William Wallace and finally obliterated in 1314 by Robert the Bruce who: *'had it razed to the foundations that it might no longer serve the English as that it had done'*.

Gracing the foot of St Paul's, standing near the site of his birth place, is a bronze statue of **Admiral Lord Viscount Duncan** (1731-1804). Admiral Duncan became a hero in 1797 when he destroyed a Dutch naval fleet, thus thwarting plans by French emperor Napoleon Bonaparte to invade Britain.

The French were threatening to overrun Europe. They defeated the Dutch and had pressed Holland's fleet into service. A powerful legion of some 35,000 French troops were poised to invade Britain by sea. Meanwhile across Britain a mutiny had erupted and the British fleet was soon immobilised. Hope turned

Statue: Admiral Duncan was born in Bluebell House which was situated in the Seagate.

to Adam Duncan who dispatched to Texel, on the north-west coast of Holland, with orders to blockade the Dutch fleet. But so serious was the mutiny, that when he sailed, only one other warship followed his flagship 'Venerable' to sea. Duncan anchored

> Admiral Lord Viscount Duncan of Camperdown was born in Dundee on 1st July 1731. In a naval career spanning fifty-four years, he saw early service in the search for Prince Charles Edward Stuart off the West Coast of Scotland and afterwards with the Royal Navy in the Mediterranean, America, West Africa and Cuba.
>
> In his later years, he earned wide respect for his handling of the serious naval mutiny of 1797 but achieved his greatest fame through his remarkable defeat of the Dutch fleet under Admiral de Winter off Camperdown on 11th October 1797, thus thwarting a possible invasion by French and Dutch troops.
>
> He was made a Viscount on 17th October 1797 and died on 4th August 1804. In the words of Admiral Lord Nelson "The name of Duncan will never be forgot by Britain and in particular by its Navy".

Plaque extract: attached to Adam Duncan's statue in the Seagate.

the ships in full view of the Dutch Navy, and in a brilliant and daring bluff, spent several weeks signalling to what Dutch commanders thought was a vast British naval presence. This pretence was admirably kept up until the mutiny subsided and substantial reinforcements were readied for sea. On October 11th Duncan confronted and conquered the Dutch fleet seven miles off the shore of a small Dutch village called Kampen, from where the battle (Camperdown) took its name.

In the shadow of the Viscount's statue, placed in the boundary wall of St Paul's Cathedral, is a tablet signifying **Sir William Wallace's** (c1274-1305) stay in Dundee around 1287-1288. The plaque proclaims: *'Near this spot William Wallace struck the first blow for Scottish independence'*. Victim of *'the first blow'* was the tyrannical son of the commander of the English garrison. The young Wallace struck his opponent dead with his dagger, then:

Plaque signifying Sir William Wallace's links to Dundee.

'made a pair of clever heels and so escaped from the South'ron chiels'

Blin' Harry (1440-1492) the Minstrel, *'The Wallace'*.

This incident was to mark a critical moment in Scottish history and William Wallace, soon gathered round him a band of followers to help him in his work for Scotland's freedom.

Ultimately, these efforts ended when Wallace was betrayed through the jealousy of the nobles, and was carried to London where he was hanged, drawn and quartered on 23 August 1305.

Turn left into **Castle Street** and stroll down memory lane. This street has great charm with its small traditional shops and cobbled road. Here you will find **Braithwaites Coffee Merchants** which has changed little since it first opened for business in 1868. The first coffee house was opened in 1652, in London and this new luxury drink soon swept across the country - tea was to remain an expensive novelty for some time.

At the bottom of Castle Street is Shore Terrace, where the **Dundee Farmers' Market** was launched in 1999 (now it is held in Reform Street; normally held once a month, eight months a year, though check with Tourist Office for dates) and sells fresh foods and locally grown produce.

Incidentally, in the old days, this was the site of the Greenmarket and **The Lady Mary Fair**. Stalls then would have sold flowers and fruit, sweets, second hand clothes, new linen, pots and pans, meat and fish and a '*tuppenny*' would buy a saucer

Opposite '*Faer Company*' at the launch of the Dundee Farmers' Market, Shore Terrace in 1999.

The **musical heritage** of Dundee has been likened to that of the American South: work in jute mills being similar to the Mississippi cotton fields. Work was exhausting, back-breaking and poorly rewarded and in a need for escapism, music was used to express worker's experiences, hardships and sorrows - '*Their songs were delivered with raw emotion, even aggression, and were full of soul.*' Modern bands emerging from the city include: the Average White Band and the Associates.

Britain's biggest free **blues festival** first began shaking and soothing the public's soul in 1995. Held in various venues throughout Dundee city centre, it has grown into a legendary extravaganza of live bands, boogie, rock and roots music and is usually held over the summer in July. This event now attracts around 10,000 music fans, to more than 120 live performances in 30 different venues. Dundee definitely delivers a feel-good buzz and this festival is not to be missed!

of peas and vinegar from the buster stall. The street fair, with shooting range and fair ground rides, would have had barefooted children shrieking with delight. Musical recitals were performed by fiddlers and organ grinders.

In the eyes of some, the Lady Mary Fair, had become outdated and *'was no longer ... any useful purpose in an expanding city where there was a wish to clear away the clutter of the town's mediaeval past.'* Permanent premises where proprietors would pay fixed taxes was intended.

The Council had hoped that the Lady Mary Fair would loose it's appeal, but did not anticipate the defiance of the travellers towards any force of order. An interesting story tells; that news of what was being designed had spread through the city and on this particular day an angry crowd, made up from members of the public, converged on the High Street - their sympathy lying with the stall-holders. Around midday the fury of the roused mob erupted, and a stall placed in front of a chemist's shop was ransacked. Attacks on other shopkeepers' property followed. All traffic was stopped and one councillor was heard to declare, *"I have never seen Dundee so lawless as it is at this moment."* There is no record of anyone being seriously injured.

In due course, the demand for sites continued and permission was granted for a hall of permanent stalls. Later known as the **City Arcade.** (Though, it too, has since disappeared.) The **Forum Centre**, though, continues this tradition and is accessed off the High Street, Commercial Street and Albert Square.

Street Scene in Castle Street: its namesake is the only remaining indicator of the castle which once stood on the Castle Rock. The Street was formed through the castle rock in 1785, by force of gunpowder.

Right James Chalmers, was the originator of the **adhesive postage stamp** which saved the penny postage scheme from collapse - this ultimately being adopted throughout postal systems of the world.

In his Parliamentary Submission Chalmers, said that postmasters should be ordered to cancel every stamp with the imprint of the town of posting, and included a specimen of the cancellation with an imprint of Dundee.

Number 10, Castle Street was the business location for Dundonian, **James Chalmers** (1782-1853), a printer and book seller and the inventor of the adhesive postage stamp and franking system. In 1834, Chalmers printed postal labels or stamps with adhesive backs. His invention included; the printing, the melting of the gum, the gumming the back of the sheets, the drying, the pressing of the sheets and the cutting out of the squares. He proposed that these labels be placed on sale throughout Great Britain as an effective and simple means of postal payment.

Chalmers, in 1837, sent his ideas to a Parliamentary Committee looking into postal systems. It was a great shock to Chalmers that Rowland Hill, to whom he sent a copy of his plan, took the credit. The following is an extract from the Dundee Advertiser of 1st February, 1881; which broadcast the recognition that Chalmers deserved:

'It should be interesting to the people of Dundee, where the memory of Mr Chalmers is still cherished, and we recommend it to all who would like to see how red tape can crush the genius of invention and shower its honours and rewards upon those who adopt other people's ideas.'

The **Theatre Royal** opened in Castle Street in 1809-1810: its location, to this day, is marked by a bust of Shakespeare set in a niche in the building, high above street level.

In fact, **William Shakespeare** (1564-1616), may have performed in Dundee. In 1601, King James VI, invited a company of English players to visit Scotland. It is thought that the group included William Shakespeare. They played in Edinburgh and they played in Aberdeen and it is assumed that on the long journey between the two cities, the company rested in Dundee, and that they played a one-night stand there. The Theatre Royal closed its doors and held its last performance in 1886.

Shakespeare's Bust: Castle St.

The next few steps lead into Dundee's thoroughfare - the High Street. A mention must be given to the **Town House**, which was designed by the famous Scottish architect William Adam and stood for nearly two hundred years, from 1732-1932. It was, in its hey-day, a grand centrepiece for the High Street - in addition to being Dundee's favourite rendezvous in the ground level piazza - it also contained the Council Chamber, tramway offices and the town jail. The memory of the '*Pillars*', as it was fondly known by locals, is steeped in history.

It witnessed an attempt by the Jacobites to return to power under Bonnie Prince Charlie in 1745. Towards the end of the 18th-century it saw public protests inspired by the French Revolution. In 1803, when Napoleon threatened invasion, the provost assembled the Dundee Volunteers at its doors. Then, to complete its spicy past in 1832, rioters attempted to set fire to the building to *'burn out the Tories!'* The Town House was demolished amidst great controversy and older Dundonians still talk today of, *'the heart being ripped from the city!'* A plaque can be found in the City Square noting its existence.

Situated on the north-side of the High Street, at number 70-76, is **Gardyne's Land** (accessible along Grays Close). This structure is literally Dundee's hidden time-capsule. Jammed together behind the High Street frontage; this linked series of three unique buildings each reveal a myriad of passageways which have you, mentally whirring through time. Dating from 1560, the mid-1600s and around 1870 - of the three - the tiny 4-storey and double attic merchant's house tucked at the back, is Dundee's oldest surviving domestic building. This building is of traditional Scottish rubble-build and its important former occupants included several Dundee provosts. The larger of the two front facing buildings, is mostly of Victorian construction and retains impressive atmospheric interiors. These, Category A-listed, buildings are currently under restoration and are intended to become a city centre **back-packers hostel**.

Opposite page *'The Pillars'* plaque: City Square.

Page 34 Festivities around the Caird Hall, City Square.

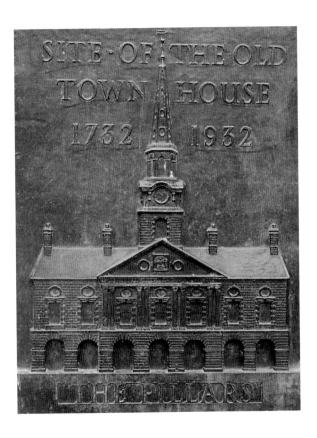

SITE · OF · THE · OLD
TOWN · HOUSE
1732 · 1932

THE PILLARS

Emerge into the **City Square** and if the weather is warm and sunny take a seat and contemplate your surroundings. Give attention to one of Britain's largest concert halls standing, gracious and poised, on the south side of the square. The **Caird Hall** bears 2,429 seats and is the major venue for pipe bands, symphony orchestras, trade fairs, galas, conferences and pop concerts. The foundation stone was laid, on 10th July 1914, by King George V and construction was completed in 1922.

Caird Hall was named after **James Caird**, (1837-1916) a prosperous jute baron of Ashton Works, who donated £100,000 (around £5 million today) towards its creation. In addition to Caird's local patriotism, (he was Dundee's greatest benefactor; paying for new medical equipment, a house and garden for the infirm, a maternity unit and a pioneering cancer wing) his generosity also paid for Shakleton's Trans-Antarctic Expedition in 1914. James also supported interests as diverse as the building of an insect house at London Zoo in 1913, acquiring rare Egyptian relics for Dundee museum and providing ambulances for the Balkan wars. Sir James, who was created a baronet in 1913, lived in an elegant home at 8 Roseangle, overlooking the Tay.

If you fancy a refreshment at this stage - there is a good choice of continental style cafes in and around the square. Locals and visitors alike enjoy eating al-fresco and, during summer months, perhaps entertained by the music and street festivities of the **'Summer in the City'** events:

'Bang-whang-whang goes the drum, tootle-te-tootle the fife.

Oh, a day in the city-square, there is no such pleasure in life!'

Robert Browning, extract '... *Down in the City'*

Pop into the Twin City Cafe, situated here in the square, and sample an exotic bite from one of Dundee's **twin cities**: the choice of authentic recipes is endless. In the years after the second World War the twinning of towns and cities throughout Europe was described as *'giving ordinary folk a chance to light candles of understanding in a dark world'*. Since 1962, Dundonians from all walks of life and ages have taken the opportunity of using the twin city links to make friends, share interests, exchange views and visits and explore commercial and trading possibilities. Dundee's twin cities include; Orleans in France, Wurzburg in Germany, Alexandria (State of Virginia) USA, Zadar in Croatia and Nablas in Palestine.

A Renaissance Statue crowning the old Clydesdale Bank - creating a theatrical effect overlooking the High Street.

An impossible-to-ignore **Desperate Dan** strides into view. Apparently, Dan is proving to be one of Dundee's most photogenic sons! Mischievously following in Dan's footsteps, is fellow '*Dandy*' and '*Beano*' characters, Minnie-the-Minx and Dawg (Dan's faithful 'mutt'). Prankster Minnie, catapult at the ready, mimics a jubilant '*tee hee hee you'll never catch me!*' Desperate Dan is one of the best loved cartoons created by Dudley D. Watkins (1907-1969) for the D.C. Thomson publishing empire.

Other public art on display here include, models of Cox's Stack, the Wishart Arch and the now demolished Royal Arch. It is worth noting that the **Royal Arch**, (originally sited in Dock Street) was especially constructed in 1844, in wood as a temporary structure, this being replaced in stone in 1851, for Queen Victoria and Prince Albert to walk through after their landing in port whilst on a visit to Dundee.

Leading off the High Street is **Reform Street**, a rare example of a Georgian Classical Terrace: having shop-fronts uniform and symmetrical

Above Dan & Co: larger than life bronze characters. In answer to the Victorian need for elaborate street furniture, blending into equally elaborate streetscapes; a new trend of contemporary decoration has appeared - with humour and originality.

Below Eating al-fresco: City Square.

Left *'Headlines'* from the Glasgow Daily Record of Thursday, December 6, 1917, declaring Churchill's success in his bid for candidature of Dundee. Sir Winston Churchill, one of the 20th century's greatest political figures, was an M.P. for Dundee between 1908 and 1922. (Article courtesy of the Daily Record.)

Right Model of the old Royal Arch: no longer exists - the arch was demolished to make way for the Tay Road Bridge in the 1960's.

with stuccoed, pilastered elevations. A casual walk to the end of Reform Street - so named after the Reform movement, whereby many a Scottish burgh renamed one of its principal streets to commemorate the passing of the Reform Act of 1832 - will include a pit stop midway, at Bank Street.

Bank Street exudes a sophisticated air with its few lifestyle shops and restaurant, and is now a bona-fide area. Though some time ago it was here that the notorious **Kinnaird Hall** once stood, and through its high arched roof a suffragette was lowered to embarrass **Winston Churchill** (1874-1965) during his candidature for Dundee West. It is an interesting point to note that working class women formed the bedrock of the **suffrage movement** in Dundee: *'I canna see why a woman who is clever enough to earn money to pay her taxes like a man, canna go and put a cross on a sheet of paper once every five years.'*

This lap of the tour now swings left into Meadowside, then left again into what can be no better an example of the past pulsating its way into the present. Pass through the gates of the **Howff** and you will uncover the relic of an old burial ground in use for 300 years. You may be astonished to find these grounds used as a lunching spot for local office and shop workers. Not the most glamourous setting perhaps, but its popularity being an escape from the urban stress - like entering a secret garden - it offers peace and tranquillity in a setting amidst mature trees and features an engaging show of daffodils and blossom in the spring and summer time.

The Howff is a fascinating place and provides a tangible insight into Dundee's Mediaeval history. Monuments and stones date from 16th to the 19th centuries and each tombstone tells a story; recalling the social history of the family, as well as illustrating changing styles and fashion. Most of the epitaphs were written as verses (not popular on gravestones today) and many show a quirky literary talent:

Now we have reached the heavenly
shore.
These mortal frames we need
no more.
Their work is done the grave
devours.
And now these Frames are no
more ours.

Dundee's Howff is one of the important Scottish grave yards. This ground was formerly occupied by the gardens and orchards of the Franciscan Friary, founded by Devorgilla, mother of John Baliol. The grounds were granted for use as a burial ground in 1564 by Mary Queen of Scots. The new burial ground was to replace the overcrowded and insanitary St Clements Kirkyard in the centre of the old burgh. An extract from the Queen's licence of 1564 states:

We, understanding that the kirkzarde of oure burgh of Dondei is situat in ye mtddis, yairof, quhairin ye comone traffique of merchandice is usit; And als ye deid of oure said haill burt is buryit; And throu occasioun of ye said buriall pest and uther contagius seikness is ingenerit; And efter infectioun it makes ye sam tp perseveir and contineu to ye Inhabitants of oure said burt bot alsua of ye haill Realme.

Right Howff tombstones are notable for their individuality - most of the epitaphs are written as verses. A volume of photographs, depicting tombs - once intact - is held in the Alexander Wilson Bequest at the Local Studies Department in **Dundee's Central Library** (Wellgate Centre).

Alexander Wilson, who was a calender manufacturer (roller-machine cloth) and lived in the Nethergate, was also a semi-professional photographer. On his death in 1923, he donated the largest part of his collection - over 5,000 glass negatives - to Dundee Public Libraries. This collection, which spans 1870's to 1905, captures the old Dundee, much of which has since disappeared.

Other collections for public view include:
Photopolis (images of Dundee 1880-1910)
James Bowman Lindsay (Bi-centenary 1999)
Rare books and manuscripts collection
Wighton Collection (of old Scottish music)
William McGonagall Collection
Tay Bridge Disaster
Ivory Collection (of approx. 300 scientific books, dating from 16th-century)
Mary Slessor Collection (of books and letters)
Lamb Collection (of 450 boxes of ephemera, mainly from the latter 19th-century)
Family History Collection

In Scots, the word '*houff*' means a meeting-place, and it was used to describe the burial ground because the **Incorporated Trades of Dundee** met here to conduct their business. However, they had previously met in the courtyard of the old Grey Friar's Monastery and the new burial ground - although a strange combination - proved to be adequate in its dual capacity.

The '*Nine Trades*', as it is referred to (included; weavers, tailors, shoemakers, glovers or skinners, bakers, fleshers or butchers, dyers, bonnetmakers and

hammermen), probably date back to the Middle Ages when craftsmen following the same occupation banded together to protect the skills of their craft from outsiders and support fair competition.

Initially, the various trades had appropriate parts of the cemetery for their exclusive use and probably met at gravestones associated with their former members. Then, in January 1581, an agreement uniting the Nine Trades into one organisation was signed, and this new association gathered at a meeting stone. The craftsmen referred to this place as '*The Stone*'.

Stone Details In The Howff
Opposite page Winged cherubs: indicating child mortality.

Right A baker's grave: many of the symbols - badges, livery and banners - associated with the different Trades are copied onto the tombs of their former members.

Ornate Entrances In The City

Left Keystone: entrance into the old Tay Hotel.

Below The old post office in Meadowside: its interior is now transformed into a trendy bar.

Opposite page right Sculpted figures on the Barrack Street Building: sculpture confers status on a building - its presence endows it with art and meaning. This building was formerly Dundee's Central Reading Rooms.

Opposite page left Sculptured details of Literature and Justice by Albert Hodge, decorate the Meadowside entrance to the D.C. Thomson & Co. Ltd., publishing headquarters.

Having absorbed the history, leave the way you came in. Opposite is the 'Courier Building'; the headquarters of **D.C. Thomson & Co. Ltd**. This red sandstone building was erected in 1902 as a public demonstration of the firm's strength and its American style was probably influenced by one of its two architects, Wigglesworth, who travelled to America to study the William Randolph Hearst empire. The other architect was David Niven, who came from Angus.

The D.C. Thomson, publishing empire began with the production of penny magazines for women mill workers and which, in 1866, produced the first half-penny morning newspaper in Britain. Their flagship, 'The Courier and Advertiser', derives from two opposing papers: the radical

Above *'The Tully'*: Dundee's local evening news.

Opposite *'The Courier and Advertiser'*: D.C. Thomson's flagship sits comfortably with other broadsheets.

'*Dundee Advertiser*' founded in 1801 '*to establish a paper in which the liberal sentiments of the people could be freely expressed*', and the Conservative '*Courier*'.

The company these days, is as much famous for its comics, and characters such as Oor Wullie, The Broons, Desperate Dan, Biffo the Bear and Lord Snooty. The dynasty today produces more than 200 million magazines, newspapers and comics each year.

Remembering the old Dundee adage: '**The Three J's**' (Jute, Jam and Journalism), where these three industries shaped Dundee's culture - though now, the former two having died to world competition, it seems journalism is the only surviving 'J'.

Pursue the trail west, pausing to admire the grand building on the corner at **Barrack Street**. This Baroque building, originally Dundee's Central Reading Rooms, was built in 1911 by City Engineer and Architect **James Thomson**. It was later occupied as Dundee's natural history and local wildlife museum (these displays now being held in the McManus Galleries and Broughty Castle Museum) but in recent times has stood unused. Curiously, Barrack Street was formerly known as Burial Wynd and in April 1807 its residents - perhaps not surprisingly - petitioned the Town Council to have the name changed. This street still echoes an unearthly feel!

A pause at **Courthouse Square** is next en-route. A scan in a clockwise fashion will show first; the '*Sally Army*' hostel built in 1851, while lining the top of the square, lies a classical courthouse as bold and beautiful as can be found anywhere. The Sheriff Court Building, built in 1833, displays a pavilion, portico and wings.

Above Warning, there is so much to absorb that a whole day would be a realistic calculation when planning a visit to Verdant Works.

Below A token linking Dundee's jute industry with the Indian subcontinent: motif on the old mill gates in Thistle Street.

Stop! On meeting the dual carriageway at the Marketgait cars by the hundred shriek by. Cross carefully and proceed along Guthrie Street. Here history greets you. Straight away you are aware of the industrial heritage - of architecture attired with age and toil. This area was the heart of the *'Jute City'*: turn third-right into West Hendersons Wynd, where a sign guides the way to Verdant Works.

Verdant Works is a gem of a visitor centre that simply defies belief! This authentic mill recreates an intensely personal journey into Dundee's jute culture. As a museum of Dundee's Textile Industries it unravels a web of kinship; linking the jute trade, ship and whaling industries, with the Indian subcontinent. It also animates the social conditions of life for mill workers. The displays and films heighten all the senses to bring alive the glories of a time few of us would ever have imagined existed. Not surprising - Verdant works was awarded Europe's Best Industrial Museum in 1999/2000.

A march straight ahead along West Hendersons Wynd and Smellies Lane surfaces at Lochee Road. Cross over and pass through an iron gate and climb a twisty stair - keeping eagle-eyed for an old drinking fountain. On reaching the top of the stairs, the castle, like a jack-in-the-box, pops into view. The eye-catching group of conical rooves and white-harled walls of **Dudhope Castle**,

Right A once, well-used drinking fountain makes a charming entrance into **Dudhope Park**: a simple beauty enhanced by the ravages of time. Such pleasures can still be enjoyed but may well not be with us for much longer.

Following page *'Fairytale'* Dudhope Castle - you almost expect Rapunzel to appear at one of the windows.

which was built around 1600 on the remains of an earlier structure, tell an ancient and varied history.

Alexander Scrymgeour, a loyal lieutenant and friend of William Wallace, was awarded, a grant of *'the upper field of Dudhope' in 1298*. (The Charter of that gift, signed by Wallace, is said to be preserved in the archives of Dundee.) The Scrymgeour family, whose name originated from *'Skirmisher'*, held the post of Constable of Dundee from 1298-1668, and were probably responsible for the rebuilding of the original stronghold and developing an extension of the earlier towerhouse, perhaps in reflection of the rise in prominence of the family, in the later 16th and 17th centuries.

In 1668 the title lapsed and the lands passed out of Scrymgeour possession. Possessed briefly by Charles Maitland, third earl of Lauderdale, it was sold in 1684, to **John Graham of Claverhouse**, Viscount Dundee (c1649-1689). It was from Dudhope in 1688, that Graham, *'Bonnie Dundee'* (or *'Bluidy Clavers'* to his enemies), started his cause in support of King James VII and II against William of Orange. The following year he raised an army in the Highlands but died at the Battle of Killiecrankie in the hour of victory. The citizens of Dundee shed no tears over his death. As Constable of the town he had been a hated tyrant.

The post of Constable was abolished in 1748. The castle declined, and was converted into a woollen mill. Around this time the English control of the Scots was strongly manifested in the terms of the Union. Woollen cloth was forbidden to be exported from Scotland, whilst the exportation of undressed wool was encouraged. That act completely crushed the woollen trade of Dundee. The factory in 1793, became bankrupt, and by 1799 it had become a Government Barracks, serving until 1880.

At the outbreak of the First World War in 1915 the castle became a barracks once again, and it was from these buildings that the **Fourth Battalion Blackwatch** left, on 23 February 1915, for France and the Battle of Loos, where the majority of soldiers perished. These recruits were mostly jute workers and D.C. Thomson employees and the loss of lives touched every home in the city.

The castle was restored in the 1980's by Dundee District Council and today it is the Business School of the **University of Abertay**. It seems natural to stroll into the castle gardens, known locally as the

'Pleasance' - you can almost sense the ghosts of the past following you.

Position yourself by the cannon, located on the south facing perimeter. From this lofty position there is a dramatic view of the city: beneath and beyond, expanding to the west, beholds an archive of visions. This is the Blackness and is one of the earliest urban industrial areas in the whole of Scotland. From the 1790's textile mills and works were built here to take advantage of the **Scourin' burn**. The burn has since been enclosed, its braes removed and the ground levelled off, though a well has been preserved and can be viewed from the courtyard of Verdant Works.

Many important sites and examples of industrial architecture still survive; though mills these days have found many alternative uses, varying from quality housing, something which their past workers did not have, to warehouses and nightclubs. Existing street names such as Brewery Lane, Smellies Lane and Horsewater Wynd, project a sense of nostalgia; making it easy to create your own perception of the industrial age - here you come back to something that has little changed.

Having recharged your batteries, leave the park through the east-exit on Barrack Road. The final stretch arrives at Euclid Street where **Dundee High School** lies

Opposite Dundee's **Time Gun** was fired daily at 1 pm until 1916. After 1924 it was used only on New Year's Day and Armistice Day, until its final crack in 1936.

Following pages 54 Portico: Dundee High School.

55 McManus Galleries: Sir George Gilbert Scott was proud of his design; referring later of Glasgow University *'I adopted a style which I may call my own invention, having already initiated it at the Albert Institute in Dundee. It is simply a 13th- or 14th-century secular style, with the addition of certain Scottish features peculiar to that country in the 16th century ...'*

ahead. Your first sight of the school is a quietly impressive one: a giant, eight-columned, Doric portico hauls itself up in Greek revival style. Mighty, weathered and worn, the building's existence in 1832, was due to an amalgamation of three older educational establishments namely; the Grammar School (a mediaeval church foundation), the Academy, and the English School. This amalgamation was known collectively as the Dundee Public Seminaries.

In 1859, a Royal Charter established the Corporation of the High School of Dundee as the governing body of the school. Until the Education Act of 1872, this school was the only provider of secondary education in the city.

Then, in 1874, local businessman (baker by trade) and philanthropist, **William Harris** (1806-1883), set out to remedy the shortage of subsidised secondary school places in Dundee. Harris offered £20,000 to benefit the High School and £10,000 to build a new academy which was to be named after him. Harris Academy opened in the west end in 1885, two years after his death.

Two of Dundee High School's famous pupils include, the 16th century historian **Hector Boece** (1465-1536), a native of Dundee whose

'*Chronicles of Scotland*' were written in Latin and published in 1525. (These were one of the earliest Scottish histories.) The other scholar - as history recalls - was Scotland's greatest Patriot, **Sir William Wallace** (c 1274-1305), who refused to recognise the sovereignty of Edward I.

It was probably whilst at this school, the young Wallace formed acquaintance with the Scrymgeours and other gallant knights and gentlemen who fought so bravely by his side against the English.

There is a choice of finishing the walk: a tour of McManus Galleries, or a welcome seat by the floral gardens at **Albert Square**. If you choose the latter, feel free to muse upon; Rabbie Burns, Queen Victoria, George Kinloch and James Carmichael.

Go and gaze upon **Robert Burns** (1759-1796). You may be forgiven for a sudden desire for America, as this bronze is the spit of Sir John Steel's statue in New York. Its location in,

...Central Park, it is lovely to be seen,
Especially in the summer season when its shrubberies
and trees are green;
And the Burns' statue is there to be seen,
Surrounded by trees, on the beautiful sward so green;

Extract: '*Jottings of New York*' by William McGonagall, (1830-1902) - Dundee's infamous poet.

Dundee's own statue was erected in 1880, at the cost of 1000 guineas (the money being raised by means of a bazaar.) The design depicts Burns meditating on his lost Highland Mary and a quotation from '*Mary in Heaven*' is inscribed on one side of the pedestal.

Next, standing proud, is **George Kinloch** (1775-1833), the '*Radical Laird*'. Fifty years after his election as MP his statue was erected to '*commemorate a signal triumph of political justice!*' On the north side and sometimes overlooked, is the statue in memory of Dundonian, **James Carmichael** (1776-1853), a great engineer and the inventor of the fan-blast.

Above Frieze: band of figurative carving depicting '*life-scenes*' adorning Queen Victoria's statue, Albert Square.

Opposite page Statue: Robert Burns, in Albert Square.

Lastly, between the reformer and the inventor, is **Queen Victoria** (1819-1901), cast in bronze. Queen Victoria's effigy appears all over the country in many guises - old, young, fat, slim, beautiful and plain - this majestic artwork was created to mark her Diamond Jubilee in 1897 and was unveiled outside the '*Albert Institute*' in August 1899, by her son H.R.H. Prince Arthur, Duke of Connaught.

If deciding to investigate the **McManus Galleries and Museum**, first check out the exterior. The '*Albert Institute*', as it was originally known, was designed by Sir George Gilbert Scott, who built the main body and the famous swirling staircase, and was opened in 1867. (This whimsical stairwell inspires photographers and artists alike and there are umpteen images appearing on postcards and paintings.)

Moving inside, the interior displays collections too rich to digest. Dundee's heritage hails you at every turn. (After completion of a refurbishment programme in 2008 - there are treats promised for every room.) The Gothic Hall, on the ground floor, welcomes you first, with the history of the building and its famous architect. On the first floor, the Victoria Gallery, which is an original feature of the Albert Institute, hosts a stunning collection of Scottish Art 1750-1914, boasting several seascapes by William McTaggart and works by local landscape painter, James McIntosh Patrick. Other works include Landseer and Millais and Pre-Raphaelite painting '*Dante's Dream*' by Rossetti. Also on the first floor a fascinating collection of material acquired by Dundonians who travelled and made their mark on the world, is set within the grandiose Albert Hall. Most captivating of all, 'Landscapes and Lives,' displays the geological, natural and archaeological area of Dundee and its environs. This theme continues through the 'Making of Modern Dundee'.

The '*Albert Institute*' was dedicated as a tribute to Queen Victoria's late consort, Prince Albert, and was established to promote science, literature and the arts in Dundee. These galleries were renamed the McManus Galleries in 1984 in memory of a former Lord Provost and is Dundee's lasting memorial to the Victorian era. Incorporating what has been described as the finest memorial to Prince Albert outside London, the McManus Galleries and Museum is now a Grade I-listed building of outstanding national importance. Fortunately, McManus Galleries also features a welcoming tea-shop, which offers light refreshment and space for reflection on the days walk.

END OF WALK ONE

CULTURAL PEPPERPOT

" Aye 'twas the train. From the southern bank

It dashed through the storm with clang and

with clank.

And Johnnie spake - 'Tis our bridge. I know:

But why do we quiver and tremble so?

More fuel, more steam! 'Gainst the storm we

strain...

... Then the wild wind's wrath became fierce and

keen.

And a flash like a thunderbolt was seen:

It glowed o'er the water with glory bright.

Then sank 'neath the waves

- and all was Night! "

THEODOR FONTANE, (1819-1898) '- *and all was Night*'

A translated extract by German poet Fontane. The Tay Bridge Disaster in 1879 inspired poets far and wide.

Opposite Victorian Bandstand, Magdalen Green.

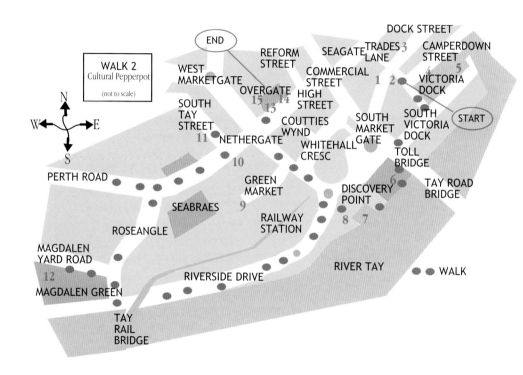

WALK 2
Cultural Pepperpot
(not to scale)

N
W · E
S

DOCK STREET

END

REFORM
STREET

SEAGATE TRADES 3
LANE

CAMPERDOWN
STREET

WEST
MARKETGATE

COMMERCIAL
STREET

1 2

4 5
VICTORIA
DOCK

OVERGATE HIGH
STREET

15 14
13

SOUTH
TAY
STREET

COUTTIES
WYND

SOUTH
MARKET
GATE

SOUTH
VICTORIA
DOCK

START

11 NETHERGATE

WHITEHALL
CRESC

TOLL
BRIDGE

10

PERTH ROAD

GREEN
MARKET

DISCOVERY
POINT

6

TAY ROAD
BRIDGE

SEABRAES

9

RAILWAY
STATION

8 7

ROSEANGLE

RIVER TAY

WALK

MAGDALEN
YARD ROAD

12

RIVERSIDE DRIVE

MAGDALEN GREEN

TAY
RAIL
BRIDGE

LEGEND

1 Sailor's Home

2 Custom House and Harbour Chambers

3 D, P & L Shipping Company

4 City Quay

5 H.M.S. Frigate Unicorn

6 Olympia Leisure Centre

7 R.R.S. Discovery

8 Old Alexandria Drinking Fountain

9 Sensation Science Centre

10 Dundee Contemporary Arts

11 Repertory Theatre

12 Victorian Bandstand

13 Mercat Cross

14 St Mary's Tower and City Churches

15 Overgate Shopping Centre

LOCATION, LOCATION, LOCATION! A SIGNIFICANT ADAGE TO QUOTE PERHAPS, KNOWING HOW OUR TOWNS REFLECT AND INFLUENCE OUR INDIVIDUAL IDEOLOGIES AND EVEN OUR personalities. Dundee's location offers the best of three environments - urban, green-lands and the river. This walk explores these spaces and presents an idiosyncratic vision of the streets, made almost tangible by witnessing first hand, the community's interests and culture.

Start at the spot marked by the anchor - aptly defining Dundee's love affair with the sea. Here you are met with a maritime theme which oozes from the buildings that circle your very position. **The Customs House and Harbour Chambers**, built in 1842-1843, was one of the largest Customs Houses in Scotland. This impressive classical building was a mark of Dundee's growing prosperity in the 19th century, and today, it is still the home to the Harbour Authorities, now the Port of Dundee Ltd. Local rumours whisper of a haunted past in the attic!

The now unused **Sailor's Home**, Unicorn House, built in 1881, stands opposite - here was a sanctuary to keep visiting sailors from *'temptation and robbery'* - when bars and brothels were abundant. Founded to provide for the physical, moral and spiritual well-being of the ship-mates - there was even a mission chapel at the back which incidentally, still stands, though derelict. Check it out. The captains stayed at the very top, in the classier rooms. What secrets lurk within these walls of yesteryear survive only in the imagination today. Look at the top of the building; illustrated are the names of famous seafarers, including Dundee's own Admiral Duncan.

The **D. P. & L (Dundee, Perth & London) Shipping Company**, formed in 1826 for the *'conveyance of goods and passengers between the Tay and London, Glasgow and Liverpool'*, can be sighted next along Dock Street. The original fleet of sailing sloops and scooners was soon added to with steam and motor vessels until the company

Above D. P. & L. Shipping Company

Opposite Sailor's Home

dominated the coastal trade. The company still operates from these premises.

The presence of these buildings remain as inspiring monuments which echo of an old Dundee, and are symbols of an important piece of the city's heritage. In contrast, **City Quay**, built around **Victoria Dock,** is Dundee's newest pedestrian retail attraction. The original dock was built from 1833 to a design by the famous engineer, **Thomas Telford** (1757-1834). Covering an area of 10.7 acres, it is still one of the largest enclosed docks in Scotland.

Left Nautical Carving: Sailor's Home. Even in the early days Scotland had a navy to be proud of and had renowned naval heroes. In 1490, one such hero, **Sir Andrew Wood**, (c 1450-1515 or 1538) who lived in Fife - was to participate in a great naval fight with the English, which was to culminate in glory for the Scots and the battle finishing in the Tay.

The story begins in a naval formation, consisting of 3 vessels under the leadership of Stephen Bull, and was dispatched from England to ambush the Scots. A brave Andrew Wood, even with only two ships, the *'Flower'* and the *'Yellow Carvel'*, was not afraid to face the English pirates and met the English squadron near the mouth of the Firth of Forth.

The tale states, that the battle begun on an August day and it raged fiercely until night set in. At daybreak on the following day the fight was renewed with fresh determination. The opposing vessels ran against each other, and the men fought hand to hand. Locked together and left to themselves, and by stress of the current, drifted round the coast of Fife until they entered the Firth of Tay. The stubborn courage of the Scots ultimately gave them the victory over the English. Wood brought his ships and prizes to Dundee, where he was greeted with a feast and honoured by Dundee's citizens.

Opposite Page H.M.S. Frigate Unicorn - figurehead.

Page 68 Top H.M.S. Frigate Unicorn.
Bottom Olympia Leisure Centre: boasts five water slides, waves and a rapid river.

Page 69 Tay Road Bridge and monument.

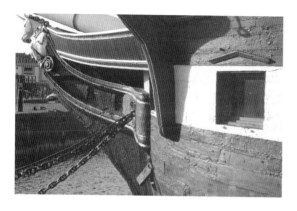

It is with delight, when you suddenly spot - in its moorings - **H.M.S. Frigate Unicorn** (launched in March 1824). This classic sailing frigate was the equivalent of the modern cruiser - *'fast and rakish'* - yet still large enough to carry a useful armament, and it proved to be one of the most successful warships of its time. Externally she appears a traditional ship, similar to Nelson's famous flagship H.M.S. Victory, yet structurally she bears the design innovations of the birth of the Industrial Revolution. The Frigate Unicorn is now the most completely original wooden sailing ship in the world and the oldest British-built ship afloat. The Unicorn is open to the public: feel free to tread across the draw-bridge for a closer inspection.

Having viewed the Unicorn's unique timber construction, pick up a pace and aim west along the

river path - the target being the monument commemorating the opening of the **Tay Road Bridge**. Her Majesty Queen Elizabeth, the Queen Mother unveiled the bridge on August 18th, 1966. It was announced: *'With the completion of the £5,000,000 Tay Road Bridge the two great estuaries of the Forth and Tay cease to be a barrier to commerce'.*

On the river trail passing behind the hotel and beyond the **Olympia Leisure Centre**, you will discover a proud symbol of the old century magnificently surviving in the new. Here R.R.S. Discovery is berthed in all her glory.

Royal Research Ship, Discovery, is the Dundee-built ship which took **Commander Robert Falcon Scott** and his crew of 47 to the Antarctic in 1901, returning in 1904. Thereafter, Discovery had a long, hard and varied life until her return to her birthplace in 1986. Leap aboard and take to the helm on these famous decks!

Enter Discovery Point - a mere spit away - and uncover the secrets of Scott's first Antarctic polar exploration. An auditorium showing video and film action and innovative displays recreate the atmosphere of what life was like for the crew who survived two long winters locked in ice. The ghosts of the past become alive in a unique presentation and here you come back to a fascinating place in time.

Left R.R.S.Discovery: this ship was one of the last wooden three-masted ships to be built in Britain and the first to be constructed specifically for scientific research.

This page The old Exchange Coffee House in Castle Street: its design spoke of a prosperous and confident local economy. This neo-classical building's original purpose was a coffee house, assembly rooms, merchants' library and reading room, and was built in 1828.

Opposite top centre Model of the '*Pillars*', on a clock situated above shop frontage in the High Street. The Town House, at the time, was considered a triumph in architecture.

Opposite top right Clocktower Warehouse, City Quay. This six-storey Italianate style warehouse, built in 1877, was originally a granary and general warehouse. Warehousing was important because it meant merchants could buy goods when the price was right then store them until they could be sold for a profit. Now it is to be remodelled into luxury accommodation.

Opposite top left Nautical clock decorating the entrance to D. P. & L. Shipping Company in Dock Street.

Opposite bottom Dudhope Castle.

Clocks in the City

Clocks and clock towers had a function - they told their own hour in an age when time was not standardised. Dundee's well loved clocks give the city its timeless appeal and charm.

Adjacent to Discovery Point, is the **Alexandria Drinking Fountain**. It is with wonder - considering today's isolated location - that this drinking fountain (now existing as ornamentation, than of practical purpose) was formerly one of the city's most popular meeting places.

Then, in the old days, folks would dress in their best attire and stroll along the promenade: *'Promenading and ha'en a gossip'* being amongst the favourite free pastimes.

The fountain was presented by Lord Provost William Longair to commemorate two Royal visits to Dundee in 1907 and 1908. It is interesting to note that during the Victorian era, drinking fountains were viewed as, *'a wholesome substitute for beer or other drink'* and the presence of fountains or pumps in the streets claimed to, *'save men from drunkenness'*. The Victorians built, literally, hundreds of them.

There is now an option to include an additional jaunt along the Esplanade, making a circuit and later rejoining your fellow walkers, otherwise venture north along Marketgait. If you are interested in science of the senses, and want a fun time, visit **Sensation**, Dundee's Science Centre: take a left turn into Green Market, where an unusual artwork - a 9.6 meter high glass seed prism - landmarks this attraction.

Cherub: Alexandria Drinking
Fountain

On deciding upon the extra mile zip up your fleece for a breezy walk. The **River Tay** is broader and deeper than the Clyde, Tyne or the Thames, and it takes approximately six hours for the tide to ebb and flow. The smell of sea-air, seaweed and salt catches your senses. Stand stock-still and listen as the gulls wheel round - lured unwittingly - you almost grasp their conversation and lose track of the here and now.

Beyond the massive girders of the rail bridge - rising in full view ahead - it is a delight to see **Common Seals** basking on the estuary sandbanks (depending on whether the tide is in or out). It is here where they give birth to their pups every June. With binoculars you will be able to identify the Common Seal: a concave forehead with nostrils forming a V-shape, almost joined at the base.

'The New Yorkers' boast about their Brooklyn Bridge,
But in comparison to thee it seems like a midge.'

The Tay Rail Bridge impressed William McGonagall to pen, *'An Address to the Tay Rail Bridge'.*

Stay at this location and look over the sea-wall, there is an eerie sensation as you identify the forsaken stumps - still clearly visible today - of engineer Thomas Bouch's ill-fated bridge, and grasp the tragic event.

On May 31st 1878, the **Tay Rail Bridge** was proudly opened. Just under two years later and on Sunday 28th December 1879, the Edinburgh train, due at Dundee station at 7.20 pm, blew into the river along with the High Girder Spans of the bridge.

Strong winds literally ripped the bridge apart and from a possible 75 passengers only 46 bodies were recovered. Not long after, Thomas Bouch died a haunted man. The events surrounding the **Tay Bridge Disaster** still hold world-wide fascination and there is a selection of artifacts held in the McManus Galleries which record the disaster: a piece of original girder, souvenirs, medals and commemorative china - a visit would quench your curiosity. The bridge was reconstructed in 1887, roughly following the same course.

If continuing the walk at the Marketgait: this area from the Nethergate leading onto the Perth Road, is a lively west-end of people at work and play. This stretch is full of pleasant art galleries, small specialist shops and eateries. It is a mecca

Left Shops, auction rooms and art galleries can be explored in Dundee's *'Cultural Quarter'*, along Perth Road.

Opposite page The exotic flavours of fine food can be readily enjoyed along Perth Road.

for antiques and collectables hunters. The cafe-bar culture thrives here; traditionally providing for the student population, it is the stylishly artistic quarter to eat mozzarella and drink lattes. An evening stroll beholds an air heady with aromas of exotic cooking: try French, Turkish, Indian, Italian - you choose. This area is buzzing!

The cultural flavour is further enhanced by both the **Dundee Contemporary Arts** centre (launched in 1999) and the **Dundee Repertory Theatre**. The DCA houses galleries, print workshops, cinemas and research facilities. The Rep - opposite the DCA along South Tay Street - has international fame as a *'nursery'* for red-hot talent and as a sounding board for new dramatists. The Rep, established in 1939, moved into this state-of-the-art theatre in 1982, and here - due to its ingenious design - *'theatre goers become the performers on a stage'*. **Brian Cox**, is probably one of Dundee's greatest thespians to emerge from the Rep. A mere lucky-dip of this *'Hollywood'* star's repertoire include - by-now-world-famous - block-busters such as *'Rob Roy'*, *'Braveheart'* and *'Troy'*.

Savour an encore before strutting on, numbers 135-139 Nethergate, require a passing mention. Here the **Morgan Tower**, dating from 1790s, has stood the test

Below Morgan Tower

Above Dundee Contemporary Arts, south elevation. The DCA is Dundee's centre for innovative, international, cutting edge exhibitions.

Page 81 The new Dundee Repertory Theatre opened in Tay Square in 1982, replacing the Nicholl Street premises which were burnt down in 1963.

of time and remains as a delightful illustration of the character of Dundee's ancient street architecture. It is notable for its five-storey bow, which projects onto the pavement, displaying its saracen's cap roof, with a crescent moon as a weather vane and its crude Venetian windows. Myth has it that these oriental designs were at the request of its original sea-captain owner, Morgan.

A short stroll will end at Seabraes where you can pause, catch a glimpse of the river views and marvel at Dundee's, '*Campus in the City*'. Here lies the hive of **Dundee University**.

The University campus consists of a blend of old and new buildings, set within a puzzle of passages, squares and extensive landscaping. Founded in 1881 as a university college, Dundee is a traditional university with a world class reputation in areas ranging from the life sciences to design. I recommend an exploration to soak up the vibrancy.

Once rested, either continue the route along Perth Road and hit the shops running - browsing for gifts, crafts or curios - otherwise turn left into Roseangle and wind your way down to Magdalen Yard Green and the Victorian Bandstand. On your way look out for **Roseangle Gallery**. This is home to the Dundee Art Society, whose principle is '*to express joy in visual arts*'. Regular exhibitions and the sale of paintings take place throughout the year. (Check local guide, acquired from libraries, or the Tourist Office, for dates)

Magdalen Green is recognised as Dundee's first suburbs: here the rich once lived behind pillared porticoes in grand Georgian houses with gardens running to the river. Later, in 1840, the fore shore was formed into

a public park by Provost Alexander Lawson. This recreation area became popular for all sorts of activities. An extract from the Programme of Events of 1944 introduces: *'All at Riverside Drive ... this fine combination of Fun Fair, Circus and Dancing, we feel sure, will be to everybody's delight, so come one and all and enjoy The Fun of The Fair'.* Great value at 6d (six old pence), for the whole shebang!

In August 1890, the **Victorian Bandstand** was erected on the *'Green'*, and in 1986, was given Listed Building Status. This cast-iron bandstand with its Victorian extravaganza, remains as one of Dundee's significant decorative landmarks. There is an aura of magic surrounding the bandstand: by way of contrast to today's modernism, its enchantment lies perhaps, in its reverence to the good old days, of rich detailing and ornate period style. These days during the summer months, the bandstand may take centre stage to instrumental musicians who might entertain audiences with a wide repertoire, ranging from brass band classics to modern chart hits.

Above Victorian Bandstand: dome detail.

Opposite Mini Bandstand, Seabraes.

Dundonian, **James McIntosh Patrick** (1907-1998), is probably Scotland's finest landscape painter and he lived in a house overlooking the '*Green*'. He was renowned for having a '*passionate love of his birthplace*', his zeal for works in and around his homelands knew no bounds and an incredible body of work exists. Members of the Royal family own pictures by McIntosh Patrick. A large oil of Glamis Castle was a wedding gift from the people of Angus to H.R.H. The Princess Margaret; while a watercolour of the Frigate Unicorn was a wedding present to H.R.H. The Prince and Princess of Wales, from the citizens and business community of Dundee. Reproductions of his work can be purchased locally, while original paintings can be viewed at McManus Galleries.

Backtrack to Seabraes for the home stretch - a saunter *'doon the toon'*. Enter the High Street and take your bearings at the town's **Mercat Cross**, situated adjacent to the Old Steeple and City Churches. The Mercat Cross features carved stone dating back to 1586, and bears on top of the column, a resin-bronze unicorn, sculpted by Scott Sutherland in the 1960's.

St Mary's Tower, or *'Auld Steeple'*, as it is fondly known, is the most ancient structure in Dundee, and is the largest Mediaeval church tower in Scotland. The existence of **St Mary's Church**, around 1190, was borne out of a vow by **David, The Earl of Huntingdon**, and his brother William The Lion, King of Scots. The Earl founded the Church of St Mary's and The King granted a Royal Charter constituting the town as a Royal Burgh and conferring The Earl as the first hereditary Provost or Constable of Dundee. The events leading to the origins of the Church are steeped in myth.

David, so the story says, at the end of the 12th-century, accompanied Richard The First of England in the Third Crusade. The crusade ultimately proved disastrous but The Earl of Huntingdon, in his retreat, then encountered a series of catastrophes. The vessel in which he sailed was wrecked on the coast of Egypt. Saved from shipwreck, he was taken prisoner and sold as a slave to a Venetian merchant. From Egypt he was carried to Constantinople where he was fortunately recognised as royalty. This recognition procured his freedom and a voyage to convey him to Scotland.

Alas, further misfortune saw his ship battered by a storm in the North Sea and narrowly escaping being run aground off the coast of Norway. In ultimate distress, the Earl prayed for his life, vowing that on whatever spot on earth he might land, he would build a church to the Virgin Mary. As it transpired, the storm abated, the craft bore up for Scotland and sailed into the Firth of Tay. The Earl landed at St. Nicholas Craig (the site of the present Discovery Point) in 1184 and true to his word founded St Mary's.

Left Street feature, at the *'Rep'*

Following page 86 City Churches - three churches in one: St Mary's and Steeple (left), St Paul's (middle) and St Clements (right).

St Mary's Church and Tower is peppered with a grim history of sackings and butchery. Records show the French chronicler, Froissart, writing that when Richard II, invaded Scotland in 1385, *'the English burned Dundee, and spared neither monasteries nor churches, but put all to flames'*. St Mary's Tower survived and the rebuilding of the church was completed in 1500. By 1548, St Mary's Church was again occupied by English soldiers; during which the church was sacked, floors of the tower burned and the bells were removed. Miraculously in 1644-5 the tower again, lived to tell another tale, when it survived a savage attack on the city by Montrose's Royalist Army.

The greatest devastation however - and the ugliest - was the siege, sack and massacre by **General George Monk** (1608-1670), in the year 1651. The town was practically wiped out as one-sixth of the population of Dundee died in its defence. During the **Civil War**, Dundee stood out for Stuart sovereignty and Oliver Cromwell had left Monk in charge of the army, with orders to take Perth and Dundee. Apparently a number of strangers from Edinburgh, Fife and elsewhere, had taken refuge in the town with their money and valuables (Dundee being the last stronghold). At least four Earls, a Viscount, fifteen Knights and many lairds had taken up their abode within the stout houses packed around Dundee's narrow cobbled wynds. The town was thus a tempting prize, and Monk was determined to win it.

Legend tells how the custom in those days was to breakfast in the ale houses and *'there being many strangers and much excitement,'* Dundonians - traditionally never one to miss a social opportunity - spent most of their time there. Soldiers too, would gather in to drink a few cups of rum and were generally drunk - as you can imagine - by noon. The story continues that Monk, supplied with intelligence from a *'wee laddie'*, became acquainted with the habits of the people and the weakness of the defenses and thus made his attack on 1st September 1651. The garrison was overpowered, though **Robert Lumsden**, the Governor, and a gallant band took refuge in St Mary's Tower and fought desperately.

Lumsden had remained loyal to the King and refused to hand the city to the Roundheads. Finding it impossible

to dislodge them from the tower, Monk's soldiers piled bundles of wet straw at its base and set the straw on fire to smoke them out. Lumsden was forced to surrender on terms; despite which, he and his comrades were double-crossed by Monk and massacred along with the many citizens who had taken refuge there. Lumsden's head - as a chiding to the locals - was severed and spiked upon one of the pointed stones on the south west corner of the tower, where the grisly remains stayed for many years.

Couttie's Wynd (off the High Street). Legend says, Cromwell's soldiers, in 1651, dragged their ill-gotten booty down these sea cobbles on the way to load the sixty ships anchored at Dundee docks.

Following this, the town was given up to riotous soldiers, who for three days and nights looted and slaughtered and then:

"Have done! Have done!" the English soldiers cried.

"Such bloody work is not for men!"

They gathered where a girlish Mother died,

And the mad butchery stopped then.

Beneath the shadow of St Mary's tower

She lay, her babe within her stiffening arms.

To-day Old Steeple sounds the passing hour

Where long ago death stormed with fierce alarums.

Salute the memory of the martyre dead -

The gentle mother whose dear blood was shed.

Anonymous

Over two centuries later, when workmen were digging in the little lane which, at the time, ran from the foot of Tally Street into the High Street, they came upon the skeleton of a woman and baby. This place was an unusual site for burial and provides extraordinary confirmation in the belief that those bones, indeed relate to the old story, dating from 1651.

Ultimately, the story of Monk ends in bizarre retribution. Sixty ships belonging to Dundee's port were laden with spoil; bails of rich cloth, silver and gold plate from mansion and church, and bound for London - but a fierce storm whipped up the Tay. Every vessel in that fleet floundered and broke up on the Abertay sands, and the valuables were lost to the sea for all time. Ironically too, Monk fell ill with a fever to the point of death and lay for six weeks in a house at the foot of the

Overgate. (This house no longer exists.)

Only the North Sea beholds the secret of **Dundee's sunken treasure**. It is estimated that £2.5 billion lies beneath the sands at the mouth of the Tay. A previous attempt to recover the wealth of 17th century Dundee failed and the 350 year old wrecks remain entombed. Dundee's beaches are a great place to visit with a metal detector!

You may enter the **'Auld Steeple'** and follow a guided tour (usually available on '*Doors Open Day*' normally held in September but check first with the Tourist Information Office for opening and tour times). If you are interested in **campanology**, you may visit the bell-ringing chamber. The belfry is fully operational and the eight bells, each weighing around seven tonnes, were installed in 1872. It is said that when The Old Pretender, father to Bonnie Prince Charlie, visited the city the original bells cracked due to the vigour with which they were rung.

The Dundee Old Steeple Bell Ringers meet here regularly and enthusiastically cheer Dundee citizens to a riotous carnival of music.

Opposite Page Old Steeple, Antiquities Room. This room contains some impressive carved stones rescued from historic Dundee buildings, including many that were demolished in the 19th century.

Right Street artist - part of the '*Summer in the City*' events.

There is an incredible urge to finish the walk with a shopping spree; considering the **Overgate Shopping Centre**, lies in your wake. The centre is busy every day and is sardine packed at weekends.

Alternatively, why not finish the walk with a cappuccino or similar beverage in one of the balcony cafe's. Which ever temptation prevails - enjoy!

END OF WALK TWO

HEL'TER SKEL'TER

" 'Twas in the month of December, and in the year 1883,

That a monster whale came to Dundee,

Resolved for a few days to sport and play,

And devour the small fishes in the silvery Tay. "

WILLIAM McGONAGALL (1830-1902) extract, *'The Famous Tay Whale'*

McGonagall, who claimed that the *'Goddess of Poetry'*, visited him in Paton's Lane, was told by the Reverent Gilfillan that *'Shakespeare never wrote anything like this'* - and took it as a compliment.

Opposite The War Memorial on the Law summit, was unveiled by Sir Ian Hamilton, on May 6, 1925.

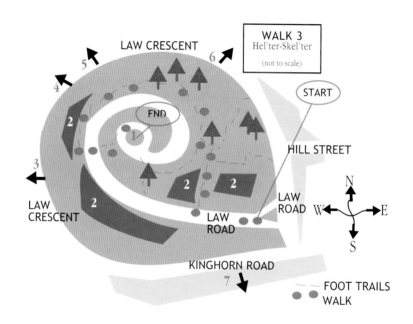

WALK 3
Hel'ter-Skel'ter
(not to scale)

LAW CRESCENT

START

HILL STREET

LAW CRESCENT

LAW ROAD

LAW ROAD

KINGHORN ROAD

FND

N
W E
S

FOOT TRAILS
WALK

LEGEND

THERE IS NO BETTER WAY TO VIEW THE FOUR CORNERS OF THE CITY OF DUNDEE THAN FROM THE TOP OF THE LAW. THIS VOLCANIC-CRAG, AT 571 FEET ABOVE SEA LEVEL boasts its own natural equivalent to the *'London Eye'*. Almost all of Dundee's landmarks can be pinpointed from here and this walk offers an enviable combination: a mini, country hike within the burning-heat of the city.

Start the ascent at Law Road and scamper a few hundred yards before turning right at Stirling Park Allotments, to follow a narrow country-style lane. Peek through the boundary fence; old and younger citizens alike, who find the freedom and retreat refreshing, toil 52 weeks a year on their horticultural patch.

Plots sprang up all over the city, and were originally given to ex-servicemen, between the first and second world wars: these men had previously been occupied as millworkers, brass-finishers, stationers, ship yard workers and ploughmen. **James Mathew** - known to many in the city as an unostentatious supporter of schemes for social welfare - had gifted £50,000 in 1935, for the purpose of placing unemployed men *'who will probably not be absorbed into industry, on the land'*. Mr Mathew, who was a Dundee Printer and Publisher and whose business published the *'Scottish Fancier'*, *'Rural Gazette'* and the *'Piper o' Dundee'*, had remarked *'If I were young and unemployed, I think I would ask for no better lot than to have a piece of ground and build my own life and fortune upon it.'*

Today, there is still a fair demand for a bit of *'grund'*. Even the smallest space, amid the jumble of plots can

One of the numerous entrances into the allotments.

produce appetising fruit and vegetables and stunning displays of flowers and shrubs.

Take the first turning left beyond the boundary fence and head along a wooded path. Keep your eyes peeled, rumour has it that the hawk, a small bird of prey, lives in these woods. Rabbits, though, are a more common sight and butterflies are a plenty. The Law provides four main **habitats for wildlife**: deciduous woodland, conifer woodland, scrubland and meadow. Tree species such as oak and hazel have been planted by local children.

Now completely shrouded by trees, turn right where the earthen-track makes a T-junction and emerge to lower views of the city. You may notice multiple small patches of vegetation smouldering (depending on the season). Do not become alarmed, this rotational 'controlled burning' encourages new vegetation and growth. Keep to the foot paths and zig-zag your way to the giddy-heights of the summit.

The **Law** exists as an extinct volcano. This area has been scoured by archaeologists and evidence of **Mesolithic Man**, a '*Hunter*', living around 6,000 BC, has been found here. On the lower slopes of the Law, ancient burials suggest its use as a religious or ritual ground, some 3,500 years ago. Archaeological digs in 1993, revealed traces of **Iron Age** occupation and a fort from 2,000 years ago. **Roman Legions** were known to have frequented the county of Angus, and the discovery of pieces of Roman pottery suggests this site may have been used as a look-out point by Roman soldiers, in the first century. Check the information panels positioned at the observation points: they depict delightful illustrations marking the history of the Law.

The unnatural flatness of the law summit is attributed to the work of soldiers who chopped off the peak to make a site for a fort. A statistical account of the town, drawn up in 1792 says, '*On top of the Law, which is the most remarkable hill in the parish, are the remains of a fortified post; the ditch is yet visible. Though the whole enclosure, which is of square form, is not of the structure with the towers which have been cemented by the force of fire, one small part of it has thus been compacted. Probably on this the fires for alarming the town were lighted, and, by frequent lighting, some of the stones have been put in to fusion.*' In place of the fort, the **War Memorial** now stands in its block-grey finery, like a stately signature - which is visible for miles around.

Above The War Memorial.

Opposite page Woody trails spiral the Law and bring an element of the rural to the city.

Amidst a cityscape; are its charms, its beauty, its humour, its people and the kaleidoscope of life that it presents. An accurate vision of Dundee was written by the poet and humorist, **Thomas Hood** (1799-1845), who lived in the town between 1815 and 1817:

Their buildings as though they'd been
scanty of ground
Are crammed into corners that cannot be found,
Or as though so ill-built or
contrived they had been
That the town was ashamed they
should ever be seen.
And their rooted dislike and aversion
to waste
Is suffered sometimes to encroach
on their taste.

For beneath a theatre or chapel
they'll pop
A saleroom, a warehouse or mean
little shop,
Whose windows - or rather
no windows at all -
Are more like to so many
holes in the wall.
And four churches together
with only one steeple
Is an emblem quite apt
of the thrift of the people.

Thomas Hood was the son of a Scottish bookseller who was sent from his birth town of London to stay with Dundee relatives to convalesce. Whilst in Dundee he wrote for the local paper. His most famous poem was *'The Song of the Shirt'*.

Opposite page Lower slopes of the Law: south facing views. These walks can reveal entirely new aspects of the city to even those familiar with it.

Cast your eyes over the panoramic views ranging as far as Carnoustie to the east, the fertile grounds of the Carse (famous for its '*rasps*' and strawberries) to the west, the rolling Fife hills to the south, and to the north, the Sidlaws and Grampians beyond. Every contour of Dundee's landscape can be savoured.

From this poetic tower it is easy to conjure images of Dundee's ancient history. The old town of Dundee begins to figure prominently in authenticated history about 834 AD, when **Alpin, the King of Scots**, made Dundee his headquarters.

In earlier centuries the country was divided into

KINGS CROSS RD.

Still bearing the name today, Kings Cross, is the location where Alpin, King of Scots was executed, around 834 AD.

two kingdoms - Pictland and Scotland, or the Kingdoms of the Picts and the Scots. The Picts were the original inhabitants. The Scots hailed from Ireland, and took possession of the Western Isles and the whole of the Western Highlands. The Picts were confined to the Lowlands, and their domains extended from the Firth of Forth northward by the coast. The Scots gradually gained on the Picts, and ultimately the Pictish Kingdom was absorbed by the Scots, when both realms were united under one King.

Historians tell that it was around 834 AD, when Alpin, King of the Scots, invaded the county of Angus.

He met the Picts near Forfar and, defeating them, marched his triumphant army southward and captured Dundee. It is believed that Alpin easily commanded the town and the castle on the rocky shore by holding the fort on the Hill (the Law).

Brudus, the Pictish King rallied his army after his defeat and the two armies met and fought on the north side of the Law. After a *'bloody clash'*, the Picts gained the advantage. Alpin was taken prisoner, and was afterwards beheaded by order of Brudus. The place where he was executed still bears the name King's Cross. The locality in which he was buried is called Pitalpin to this day, and is situated at the west of Lochee.

Zoom in and focus on specific points of interest. Pick out Balgay Hill, a wooded hillock to the west, where, hidden among the tall, tangle of trees, is Britain's only full-time public observatory, with resident astronomer. **Mills Observatory** is set in a classically styled sandstone building, with a distinctive papier-mache dome, which houses a 250 mm Cooke refracting telescope.

The Mills Observatory takes its name from **John Mills** (1806-1889), a Dundee twine manufacturer and amateur astronomer. Mills directed that his estate, *'should be devoted to the provision of a building*

Mills Observatory, is only one of its kind in Britain to have been conceived, constructed and used for the benefit of the public.

---

equipped with astronomical and other instruments suitable for the study of the wonder and beauty of the works of God in creation.' His wishes were granted accordingly and this observatory was erected, equipped and endowed by his trustees. The Observatory opened on 28 October 1935.

Budding enthusiasts can indulge in displays which cover an impressive array of physical concepts, from the Big Bang to Space Exploration. Expert advice is always on hand, so why not ask those burning questions: What is a Wormhole? A White Dwarf? A Light Year? You can also view instruments or take in a planetarium show. A glass case of effects marks the significance of **James Bowman Lindsay** (1799-1862), who is one of Dundee's most notable inventors.

The list of Lindsay's inventions and discoveries is astonishing: he invented a system of astronomical dating for history, discovered electric light, invented electric telegraphy and before his death had completed a Pentecontaglossal Dictionary which cross-referenced in fifty languages. (Languages included; English, Scottish, Anglo-Saxon, Gothic, Icelandic, Danish, Swedish, Tibetan, Manx, Hebrew, Greek, Russian, Turkish, Arabic, Bengali, Eskimo, Chinese and Gaelic.) He was reputed to have once travelled 50 miles on foot to Edinburgh to consult the Advocate's Library to obtain the correct sound and meaning of a single character in Chinese language.

In Lindsay's era, light was still a rare and costly experiment. No other pioneer had been able to produce more than intermittent flashes, but Bowman Lindsay, succeeded in 1835 in producing a constant stream of light which was one of the great wonders of the day.

The distinctive papier-mache dome of Mills Observatory.

James Bowman Lindsay was born into a weaver household and was almost entirely self-taught. He had denied himself food and clothing so that he could buy books, and his house at 11 South Union Street, was stuffed with books, inventions and apparatus. He died of malnutrition in 1862 and is buried in the Western Cemetery in Dundee. His achievements are commemorated in a biography by A.H. Millar (1925), which has a foreword by **Marconi**.

From Balgay Hill scan in a clockwise direction and settle your gaze upon **Cox's Stack**, sited in Lochee. This prominent quadrangular 280 feet landmark, was built in 1865, and is one of a few remaining legacies from the might of Dundee's jute industry. This million brick chimney - in keeping with the Victorian school of thought, *'Chimney tops are features of considerable importance'* - has the appearance of an elaborately decorated Italian campanile or bell-tower.

Lochee owed its existence to the Lochee Burn which powered the mills, and here settled a manufacturer from a bleaching family, called Cock around 1700. By 1777, David Cock had 280 hand-looms at work. Known after 1851, as the **Cox Brothers**, his descendants pioneered the production of jute cloth.

At the height of of Dundee's jute supremacy around 1864, there were 61 spinning and power-loom businesses in the city, the Cox Brothers' (James, William, Thomas and George) Camperdown Works held 200 acres (the largest jute works in the world); with its own branch railway, stables, foundry, *'half-time'* school and fire-station, and gave employment to more than 5,000 workers. The entrepreneurial spirit of William Cox and the brothers' ideology of self-sufficiency led to their owning and operating an independent carrier fleet. (In 1883, the Dundee Clipper Line was founded.) The Cox Brothers' named their firm as a compliment to their neighbour; the Earl of Camperdown.

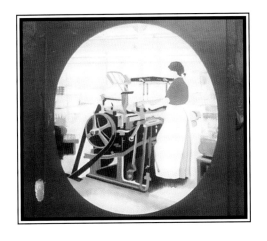

Mural from the old *Weavers Bar*, in Princes Street. Mill work was sweaty, noisy labour with dangerous working conditions and the majority of workers were women and children. This gave Dundee a new cultural identity and the city became known as a **'Woman's' town** or **'She' town**, due to the dominance of women in the labour market (as women were paid less than men). This independence obviously gave women a new-found freedom, but the responsibility of being the main provider to the family created problems, not only for the women, but for the men, who stayed at home and who became known as **'Kettle-boilers'**.

Camperdown Country Park, lies north west of Cox's Stack on the outskirts of the city. It stands, on the old formal grounds of **Camperdown House**, which was once part of a much larger estate that stretched all the way to the Sidlaws in the north. Camperdown House was constructed for the **Second Viscount Duncan**, First Earl of Camperdown, local landowner, British peer and son of Admiral Duncan.

Although the house is not open to the public, the **Camperdown House Project** (a partnership between Dundee City Council, the National Galleries of Scotland and the National Museums of Scotland) aims to restore and open Camperdown House as an historic country house and to display collections relating to the story of the Duncan family and their place in Scottish and British history. A few examples of memorabilia which could be shown, are currently exhibited in McManus Galleries.

Camperdown Park is set in around 395 acres and is probably the city's most captivating public estate. Trees include the rare weeping wych-elm and wildlife include a bear, lynx, golden eagle and wolf. Do not panic! - these creatures are housed in the park's **wildlife centre**. The park also cherishes an 18-hole golf course, pitch and putt, boating pond, childrens' adventure range and duck pond. Why not map out an additional walk of your own - what an adventure-and-a-half that would be!

Animals at Camperdown Wildlife Centre
Above European Lynx: once found throughout the continent, including Britain, but now only survives in a few isolated areas.

Opposite page Red Deer: once widespread in ancient woodlands; can still be seen on moorland, mountain areas and scattered woodlands in Scotland.

Set your sights over Dundee's harbour area. It was from here in 1797, **John Keiller,** a small-time Dundee grocer, bought a cargo of Seville oranges from a Spanish ship owner, who had taken refuge in Dundee harbour to avoid a brewing storm. Proving difficult to sell the oranges because they were so bitter, and not wishing to waste them, Janet Keiller decided to boil the oranges with sugar. Thus, in an act of providence, the first **Dundee marmalade** bubbled into life.

Opposite page Camperdown House was constructed for **Robert Pundas Duncan Haldane** (... -1859) the Second Viscount, First Earl of Camperdown. The Earl was a high-spending aristocrat with friends in the circle of the future King William IV. His new house was finished to the highest standards and had an uninterrupted sequence of state and reception rooms lining the front overlooking the garden and firth, which was designed to impress guests. Judge for yourself!

A tasty treat: these distinctive white pots were sold in millions, all over the world.

Prominent like soar thumbs: a north-easterly position from the Law, shows the position of Dundee's two **football stadiums** (belonging to Dundee Football Club and Dundee United Football Club) - this area being the centre of the universe on a Saturday. Dundee F.C. won the Scottish cup in 1910 and Dundee United F.C. won it in 1994.

The Law gifts Dundee with a unique perspective in which to view the city's mightiness in miniature. Survey the **port** area. Dating from 11th century, it began at the Seagate, finishing at the sea wall at St. Nicholas Craig. Trade gushed through this natural harbour: imports around the 15th century included wood, sail, canvas, glass and copper. From 1500, Dundee was the main port for emigration to Poland and other Baltic states and Dundee traders had permanent bases in Denmark, Germany, Sweden, Holland and Poland. Ships which took goods to Europe brought back not only onions and oranges, but ideas and philosophies. George Wishart, Dundee's famous martyr, was not the only or the first cleric to travel between Dundee and the continental universities. Dundee, as one writer says, *'may have acted as a funnel for the reforming ideas* *that infiltrated from continental Europe.'*

By the mid 17th century, Dundee's harbour must have been substantial, by virtue of the 60 vessels recorded, as having been plundered by General Monk. Again, in the 19th century, the port expanded, due to the Jute Trade from India, and the South Atlantic Whaling Trade. In 1870, 216 ships and 18 whalers were registered at Dundee docks. Here were the fortune-seekers, finders and losers whose entrepreneurial drive helped to establish the **jute and whaling trades** in Dundee. One whaler's hope and pride is immortalised in this sea-shanty:

O the noble fleet of whalers out
sailing in Dundee
Well manned by British sailors to
work them on the sea;

On the western ocean passage none
with them can compare,
For there's not a ship could make the
trip as the Baleana, I declare.

Whales in those days must have been present in large numbers though were not a common sight in the waters of the Tay. According to Thomas Jefferson the whale was, *'an active, fierce animal, requiring vast address and boldness in the fisherman.'* Imagine the excitement when, in early December 1883, a male humpback whale appeared in the Tay. (Its presence was presumably due to its following shoals of herring and sprats which were unusually abundant that year.)

Finally, on 31st December 1883, the **'Tay Whale'** was subsequently - like in Herman Melville's, *'Moby Dick'* - *'harpooned and dragged hither from the bottom* *of the sea'.* A Dundee oil merchant, **John Woods**, then purchased the floating carcass, towed it into Dundee docks and intimated: *'that when done exhibiting the monster, and after it has been dissected by learned professors, I will be happy to hand over the remains to you for presentation to the town of Dundee, so that its skeleton may be secured for our own museum.'*

Eeny, meeny, miney, mo - its tough deciding where yonder to place your vista, landmarks lay scattered like confetti. Before preparing for your descent, allow yourself time to study the views, take photographs and enjoy the sensation from this ethereal plateau.

END OF WALK THREE

The skeleton of the '**Tay Whale**' is exhibited at the McManus Galleries. Now a protected species, humpbacks are still found in all the oceans of the world, although extremely rare in British waters. These creatures were easy prey to whaling ships as they are relatively slow swimmers.

Above Views to the north from the Law.

AS PRETTY-AS-A-PICTURE

" Others may look at the northern shores of the Tay and think them dreary and black. They were not so to me then. They were the eyrie of freedom and the pleasant region where, unheeded, I could commune with the creatures of my fancy. "

MARY SHELLY (1797-1857)

Historians believe that Shelly's time in Dundee, between 1812-1814, influenced her great novel *'Frankenstein'*.

Opposite The Grassy Beach, Broughty Ferry.

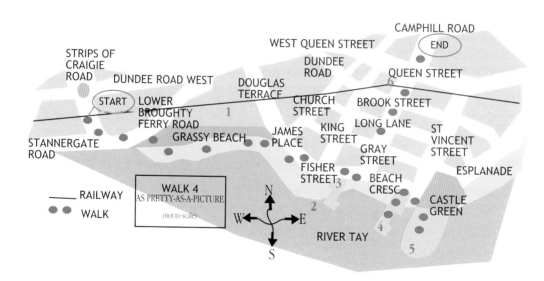

STRIPS OF
CRAIGIE
ROAD
DUNDEE ROAD WEST
STANNERGATE
ROAD

WEST QUEEN STREET
DUNDEE
ROAD
CAMPHILL ROAD
END
QUEEN STREET

DOUGLAS
TERRACE
START
LOWER
BROUGHTY
FERRY ROAD
1
CHURCH
STREET
BROOK STREET

GRASSY BEACH
JAMES
PLACE
KING
STREET
LONG LANE
6

FISHER
STREET
3
GRAY
STREET
BEACH
CRESC.
ST
VINCENT
STREET
ESPLANADE

RAILWAY
WALK

WALK 4
AS PRETTY-AS-A-PICTURE
(not to scale)

N
W
E
S

2
4
5
CASTLE
GREEN

RIVER TAY

LEGEND

THIS TRAIL FOLLOWS THE COASTAL SHORE FROM WEST TO EAST AND ENTERS THE DELIGHTFUL SEASIDE SUBURB OF BROUGHTY FERRY. THIS IS DUNDEE'S '*RIVIERA*'. ONCE RECOGNISED AS THE '*richest square mile in Europe*', this journey explores the transitional areas between city and environs: from the humble beginnings of a little fishing village; to where the wealthy jute barons built their mansions.

Begin at the old Broughty Ferry Road and lead the way eastwards, skimming the old sea wall. Firstly though, consider the area to your right, which rolls into the **Stannergate** and the old ship building yards. (Incidentally, until recently, Dundee was Scotland's ship building centre, ranking second to Glasgow.)

This area is recorded as the site of one of Dundee's **earliest human settlements**: here lay evidence of a kitchen midden, with shell-fish remains and animal bones dating around 6,500 BC. In those days, historians say, painted savages, living by primitive means of fishing and hunting would have existed naturally by the shores of the Tay.

Stray onto the beach path. This is the **Grassy Beach** and is popular with locals so be prepared for a friendly nod of the head - this being the customary etiquette of the walking enthusiast. The dog-walker pack hangs out here: poodles, peeks, cocker spaniels - all breeds - frolic in ecstasy in the shallow waters, while their owners enjoy the spectacle just as much! When the tide is out, this is a popular haunt for beach-combers, with wide-eyes peeled for a gratuitous discovery - a gold coin from Monk's wrecks perhaps or an interesting remnant of driftwood. The main

The Grassy Beach is very popular with walkers. Dundee is an intimate city, when out and walking around you are sure to come across a friend.

Dundee-Aberdeen railway line runs adjacent on your left and you are sure to be stopped in your tracks as a train hurtles by.

In the summer months you may trample the shore braes on a carpet of wildflowers; which in the autumn culminates into a state of faded splendour. Look out for **sea birds** such as the oyster-catcher; these and a variety of other waders feast in this area - you can identify waders as having long legs and a long beak which they use to probe in the sand for food.

Remarkably, the Tay Estuary holds the largest concentration of Eiders in Britain. Up to 20,000 are regularly found here in the winter, feeding on the extensive mussel-beds at the mouth of the Tay.

As the path ends and meets Douglas Terrace, pause for reflection. If luck is in and the day is sunny, then the River Tay glimmers and winks. This is a fitting reminder of words from the *'world's best worst poet'*, **William McGonagall** (1830-1902), who spent most of his time living and recording life in Dundee.

Beautiful silvery Tay,

With your landscapes, so lovely and gay

Along each side of your waters, to Perth all the way;

No other river in the world has got scenery so fine,

Only I am told the beautiful Rhine...

Beautiful, Beautiful! silvery Tay.

Extract, "*A Descriptive Poem on the Silvery Tay*" - perhaps one of McGonagall's best worst!

'*La la la, dum dum dee dum tru lu la*' - reminiscing poetry in an idyllic setting ignites the creative senses and you would be forgiven for whistling on your way.

Make a bee-line for Broughty Castle: beckoning like a mirage from afar. On the way discover fairy-tale-like-cottages clustered around the harbour once belonging to the fisher-folks. This is **Fisher Street**, the oldest part of Broughty Ferry and life began here as a little hamlet on the shores of the river. Fishing was once the '*Ferry's*' tradition. This included herring and sprat fishing and the village was also at one time, an important salmon-netting station. In the 1880's there were 180 fishermen and more than 80 boats were in operation.

Post cards showing Broughty Ferry's '*fisher life*', proved a picturesque subject over a century ago. Postcard manufacturers included, Raphael Tuck and Valentines of Dundee. '*Valentines*', later become one of the largest publishers of postcards in the world.

Around 1832, **James Valentine** (1815-1879) set up a shop in the Murraygate as photographer and fancy stationer. Business began at first for portraiture, but later also for landscape views for which the firm became, in the words of its catch-phrase, '*Famous Throughout the World.*' Queen Victoria, sharing the general enthusiasm for this new art form, commissioned James to produce a series of views of Highland scenery and granted him a warrant as '*Photographer to the Queen.*'

Hovering by the harbour is the **Broughty Ferry**

Below *'All-aboard!'* In all weathers, the **Royal Tay Yacht Club**, first established in 1875 and receiving its Warrant in 1891, are on the river in their fleet of craft.

Here, bobbing in the bay, boat-bells tinkle distinctly, making lament with the wind. The Tay estuary offers perfect and varied conditions for yachting and the Yacht Club holds regular regattas and races. Visiting yachtsmen are welcome.

Lifeboat. A lifeboat service was first instituted at Broughty Ferry in the early 18th century. The station was taken over by the Royal National Lifeboat Institution in 1861 and a boathouse was built. The present boat, which was launched in 2002, is named the *'Elizabeth of Glamis'*, in honour of the Queen mother - in recognition of her local connection and her then role as the patron of the Royal National Lifeboat Institution. The harbour is also the venue to brave (or mad) individuals participating in the *'Ne'er Day Dook'* (1st January). This is the annual **Tay crossing swim** for Ye Amphibious Ancients Swimming Club, who attempt to swim the icy waters to Tayport.

Overlooking the harbour is one of the most eye-catching private residences on the waterfront - **Barometer Cottage**. The Bell fisher family built this

Below The picture postcard industry had its home in Dundee.

cottage in 1812 and retained it until 1975. The Meteorological Society installed the barometer in its sentry in 1859, for the benefit of the fishermen of Broughty Ferry. Tales tell, on at least two occasions other fishing villages along the coast, with no barometer to warn them to stay at home, suffered drownings. Unfortunately the instrument was stolen many years ago and the sentry box alone survives.

Promenade along **Beach Crescent**, admiring numbers 9-13: these are classical Georgian houses built around 1800, and display some opulent details. Make towards the wharf at the old **Pilot Pier** and ascend the viewing tower. Fife's small harbour town of Tayport seems just an arms stretch away, on the south bank.

IN HONOURED MEMORY OF THE CREW
OF THE ROYAL NATIONAL LIFEBOAT "MONA"
STATIONED AT BROUGHTY FERRY
WHICH FOUNDERED, WITH THE LOSS OF ALL HANDS,
IN A GALE IN THE FIRTH OF TAY
ON 8TH DECEMBER 1959,
WHILE RESPONDING TO A CALL FROM THE
NORTH CARR LIGHTSHIP WHICH WAS
ADRIFT IN THE NORTH SEA.
RONALD GRANT   GEORGE WATSON
GEORGE B. SMITH   JAMES FERRIER
ALEXANDER GALL   JOHN T. GRIEVE
JOHN GRIEVE   DAVID ANDERSON

Left The '*Mona*' memorial plaque: displayed on the north wall of the boat house. The '*Mona*' served from 1935 until she was lost with all hands in a terrible storm in 1959.

Opposite page The '*resident*' swans are a popular attraction in the '*Ferry*'.

Just to your left of Tayport, at the mouth of the river, is **Tentsmuir Point** which has been a **National Nature Reserve** since 1954. Most of Tentsmuir is conifer forest planted by the Forestry Commission: red squirrels, long-eared owls and the occasional capercaillie can be seen here.

The viewing tower is a great vantage point to admire the sea and discover the bustle of the river. The Dundee Port Authority **'Pilot Cutter'** can be seen several times a day cruising the Tay escorting visiting ships safely into port.

From here, spin your sights in-land over the cityscape. Broughty Ferry looks like a structural melting pot: all styles and sizes blended together into one mosaic whole. This wall-to-wall explosion of architectural eclecticism ranges from the tiniest-ever fisher cottages, and rises up-hill, to grand mansions which were once owned by filthy-rich **jute millionaires** who accessorised their property with well-kept grounds, conservatories, stables and lodges.

Ponder on the romance of **Carbet Castle,** though now long gone the new block of flats standing in its place along Camphill Road is supposed to imitate the gothic splendour of the original Carbet Castle. The original property was built for the *'Jute family'* Grimmond, who kept on extending the house in an eccentric manner (a sport of the rich, no doubt) to rival another wealthy family, the Gilroy's, who owned **Castleroy** (also demolished). Fortunately, Carbet Castle, before its demolition (due to an attack of dry-rot), removed the fantastic painted ceilings by Charles Frechou and these were given to Dundee University's Art Faculty. The Baronial gate lodge to the castle alone survives.

Ultimately, conclude your visual whirl over the very tip of a geographical tentacle, on which Broughty Castle perches firm and stoic, like a soldier on sentry duty.

Broughty Castle was built in 1496-1498, by Andrew, 3rd Lord Gray. In 1547, Lord Gray, in the manner of a traitor, surrendered it to the English, with whom Scotland was then at war, during the Regency of Mary of Guise. Thereafter, the castle was

Right View of Camphill Road from Gray Street, looking towards Carbet Castle gate lodge.

Opposite page Beach Crescent: parading opulent details in its street features.

garrisoned with nearly 2,000 English soldiers. In 1559, the forces of the Lords of the Congregation took possession, holding the castle until 1571, when it was again besieged and taken by Seaton of Parbroath, in the interest of the Catholic faction. After this period the castle fell into ruin and lay derelict for centuries, but was rebuilt in 1860 as a coastal fortification and garrisoned by the Royal Artillery. In 1887 it was passed on to the hands of the Royal Engineers, after which, it was used for military purposes until as recently as World War II. Nowadays, Broughty Castle is a fascinating museum.

Step inside and within a split second of breathing you find yourself inhaling the mustiness of an almost tangible history. Wind your way up four floors of artifacts covering the life and times around the area of Broughty Ferry; its people, the environment and wildlife that lives close by. **Broughty Castle Museum** houses an Aladdin's cave of historical memorabilia: paintings, stained-glass, photographs, certificates, models, souvenirs, armoury - a curator's dream!

Opposite Broughty Ferry Castle: '*Square, black and grim on its rock that jutted into the Ferry*', a description used by James Grant in his novel '*The Yellow Frigate*' (a preserved edition can be found in the Local History section of Dundee's Central Library). However it is perceived it certainly evokes a lasting impression.

Opposite page Sea-sortie! Broughty Ferry harbour.

Dundee has long held a love affair with the sea. The majesty and mythology of the **whaling industry** is kept alive in both the McManus Galleries and Museum and Brought Castle Museum. The museums' collection of **whaling relics** dates mainly around the last years of the Arctic history, at a time when Dundee operated the only fleet in the British Isles. As an industry, Arctic whaling has long been of importance to the city of Dundee, the earliest company was founded about 1750. Though the associated buildings themselves are now gone, street names like East Whale Lane, Whaler's Close and Baffin Street, still indicate the city's past connections to the trade.

The lives of whaler's were very different from other men. Living at sea for up to three years; these mariners undertook back-breaking work earning only pennies a week.

A typical catch would include harpooning the whale from tiny row boats, then the men might be swept through the water at terrifying speeds of up to 20 knots. Once killed and hauled aboard, the waste piece alone - the whale's forehead - might weigh over ten tons. The vast whalers were often described as *'floating Hells'*, but this industry was lucrative and the seamen became accustomed to it.

Huge and handsome profits were made from the products of whaling; such as soap, perfume and candles. Later, while other ports suffered from a diminishing market for whale oil, due to the introduction of gas for street lighting, Dundee continued to thrive - having an alternative home-made market. With the jute industry in its infancy and crying out for a lubricant to ease the process of spinning the coarse fibre, the demand for whale oil was to continue. Both industries benefited greatly from each other.

Wow! From the museum's observation tower you are treated to a skyscraper's view of the Tay estuary and the mile long strip of Broughty Ferry's **golden beach.**

These sands were popular for sea bathing as early as the 1830's, and a chronicler recorded the Ferry as, *'having become a fashionable resort for sea bathing. The sea water here is very pure, with a clean sloping beach.'* If the weather is pleasant seize the situation as an opportunity and stroll along the promenade, or bring out the child in you and build castles in the sand, metaphorical or otherwise.

These days Broughty Ferry remains an attractive spot in which to live. A place where shops still retain the romance of individual facades and shop windows display a wide array of goods for sale.

Light Refreshment - in the Ferry Opposite page Tea-room in Gray Street - small, homely and relaxed.

This page Harbour-side hospitality. Pubs welcome Dundonians and visitors alike.

Broughty Ferry Station. The former Station Master's house, waiting room and other buildings have recently undergone refurbishment and are Category A listed buildings.

Broughty Ferry owes its sea-shore resort status to the railway and Broughty Ferry Station is one of the oldest stations in Scotland. Prior to 1838 (when the railway line opened), it was a tiny fishing village, but the railway offered an opportunity for city-slickers to escape Dundee and the industrial grime - subsequently the community of Broughty Ferry prospered as a holiday destination.

Save the best until last, and backtrack along Beach Crescent and enter Gray Street - gateway to a shopper's haven. Sample individual boutiques, art and craft shops, galleries, tea shops and fine eateries, books and floral creations - the choice is endless! I suggest amid all this shopping hullabaloo, a stop for the customary **seaside ice-cream**.

The sale of ice-cream was first popularised by Italian street vendors and confectioners at the end of the 19th century. In Broughty Ferry, confectioner, **Donald Tolonetti's Refreshment Rooms** in Castle Terrace (around 1920) was one of the earlier establishments. This by-gone cafe sold tea, coffee, ice-cream and Fry's chocolate. Today, **Visocchi's** in Gray Street, still make ice-cream on the premises using traditional Italian recipes: choices include Mint Tulip (vanilla & mint ice-cream topped with chocolate sauce, whipped cream, flake and cherry), Michaelangelo (a ceramic artists palette: any 4 scoops of ice-cream and 2 sauces) or every one's favourite, Knickerbocker Glory! Its not surprising then, that Broughty Ferry is coveted by Dundonian's, as the idyllic suburban way of life.

Broughty Ferry is very '*sea-sidey*' - and no visit would be complete without the traditional ice-cream cone.

END OF WALK FOUR

INDEX

About the author

Cambella McMahon belongs to Dundee: born and bred. She is passionate about books, photography, art, literature and life! She studied at Dundee College and Dundee University. This is her first book.

Pumpkin Press Souvenirs title in preparation, to be published late 2007:

Dew on the Law and other Strange Stories about Dundee

by Cambella McMahon.

Acknowledgments

The bulk of the research involved in the making of this book included: observation, conversation, newspaper clippings, articles, pamphlets, guides and local interest sources. A special thank you to the helpful staff at Coldside library.

Disclaimer

At the time of publication the McManus Galleries and Museum began a restoration programme and as a result will be closed until 2008. Other features of the walks in this guidebook are as described but some may change in the future.